The
Christian
use of
Time

The Christian use of Time

Niels-Erik A. Andreasen

Abingdon
Nashville

The Christian Use of Time
Copyright © 1978 by Niels-Erik Andreasen

Library of Congress Cataloging in Publication Data
Andreasen, Niels-Erik A.
    The Christian use of time.

    Bibliography: p.
    1. Time (Theology)—Meditations. 2. Sabbath
—Meditations. I. Title.
BT78.A53   242'.4   78-847

ISBN 0-687-07630-7

Scripture quotations in this publication unless otherwise noted are from
the Revised Standard Version Common Bible, copyrighted © 1973.

Scripture quotations noted NEB are from The New English Bible © the
Delegates of the Oxford University Press and the Syndics of the
Cambridge University Press 1961, 1970. Reprinted by permission.

79-4824
Manufactured by the Parthenon Press at
Nashville, Tennessee, United States of America

To Demetra

Preface

The Christian Use of Time is a series of reflections, ten in all, upon the insights and benefits that the weekly day of rest may bring to ordinary busy people. It is not a technical book, and it does not pretend to speak to the specialist in theology, philosophy, or psychology. Neither is it a doctrinal book that promotes a particular religious point of view. Nevertheless, it does proceed from a decidedly Christian premise, namely that every person, Christian and non-Christian alike, is created with the potential to lead a meaningful life. This modest book is offered in the hope that it may assist in reaching that potential. To that end it will suggest that the day of rest, inherited from the Bible and known variously as the sabbath, Sunday, or simply the weekend, deserves our careful attention once again. For a long time we have abused the day of rest, used it thoughtlessly, and wasted its potentials as a source of well-being. But now is a time for conservation, not only of our natural resources, but also of our spiritual heritage, and the day of rest belongs to the latter. On the special time of this day we are invited to contemplate our past achievements or failures, our present situation, and our aspirations for the future—in short, all the matters that occupy all our time. Hereby, the special time of the day of rest may become the pivot around which the wheel of all our time turns, and that is the suggestion of this book.

Special thanks go to students and colleagues at Pacific Union College and Loma Linda University for various acts of assistance during the preparation of the manuscript.

1
𝔉𝔦𝔫𝔡𝔦𝔫𝔤 𝔗𝔦𝔪𝔢

What Is Time?

"I do not have time" is the most common excuse we offer when our attention is requested. Generally, we do not admit to a lack in ability or in resources, but we are constantly short of time. Our daily life is so full of changes that time leaves us behind again and again. We rush from bed to breakfast, speed along the freeway to the office, then follow work, coffeebreak, work, a meeting or an errand during lunch, more work, more coffee, and finally beating the rush-hour traffic home to a full evening at the club or before the television. We have devised expressions such as "let's throw something together," "let's grab a bite," "let's get going," because we are always late, time is short, and there is much to be done.

The busy days run into short and hurried years, beginning at childhood, which impatiently gives way to short and eventful adolescent years, followed by marriage and mortgages, children and professional ambitions. Next comes the monotony of middle age, and finally the specter of retirement beckons us to a hasty retreat and to a certain end of our usefulness in a society that has no time to stop and listen to our story. To be sure, this is a caricature of our life cycle, but one that many of us have been taught to expect and from which we cannot easily escape. That is the fate of contemporary men and women, and there is apparently little we can do to alter it. We are rushed through life, and time is our major problem.

What is time? Augustine once asked this question and responded to it with a double answer: "If no one asks me, I know; if I wish to explain it to one who asks, I know not."[1] On the surface this answer may be amusing, but it also rings true, for time is indeed a difficult matter to explain.

Traditionally time has been explained as a uniform variable, that is, a kind of temporal line that advances in regular and uniform segments. Consequently, sun, moon, and stars can be anticipated at regular and fixed intervals on the time line; things take time—that is, they last from here to there on the time line—and events like birthdays and anniversaries can be fixed in time. Nevertheless, this rather manageable concept of time has been changed in the twentieth century with the eruption of relativity theories and quantum physics. No longer is time explained as a uniform variable—an extending time line, onto which events can be plotted—rather time is now seen to be itself determined by events. For example, two events, some distance apart, may occur at different times to different observers. If they are simultaneous to one observer, they are not simultaneous to a second observer who moves with respect to the first observer. Even the time-honored (!) distinction between past, present, and future is seen to merge under the scrutiny of contemporary physical theory. No longer can a specific physical state (or event) be given a precise time, and by the same token, if a precise time is given, the physical state (event) cannot be described exactly.

Time is thus still desperately difficult to explain so many years after Augustine posed his question about it.

However, this does not excuse us from living in time and from experiencing its passing. From this there is no escape. We may not know what time is when asked to explain it, but we live our lives in time, and we have practical and distinct sensations of its passing. Unfortunately, living in time and being confronted with the passing of time is not always easy and pleasant. In fact, it can be very frustrating and even oppressive. When that happens, we wish for the ability to understand time or, even better, to control it.

Lewis Carroll created this exchange about living with time between Alice and the Hatter:

Alice sighed wearily. "I think you might do something better with the time," she said, "than wasting it asking riddles with no answers." "If you knew Time as well as I do," said the Hatter, "you wouldn't talk about wasting *it*. It's *him*." "I don't know what you mean," said Alice. "Of course you don't!" the Hatter said, tossing his head contemptuously. "I daresay you never even spoke to Time!" "Perhaps not," Alice cautiously replied, "but I know I have to beat time when I learn music." "Ah! that accounts for it," said the Hatter. "He won't stand beating. Now, if you only kept on good terms with him, he'd do almost anything you liked with the clock. For instance, suppose it were nine o'clock in the morning, just time to begin lessons: you'd only have to whisper a hint to Time, and round goes the clock in a twinkling! Half-past one, time for dinner! . . ." "That would be grand, certainly," said Alice thoughtfully, "but then—I shouldn't be hungry for it, you know." "Not at first, perhaps," said the Hatter, "but you could keep it to half-past one as long as you liked." "Is that the way *you* manage?" Alice asked. The Hatter shook his head mournfully. "Not I!" he replied.[2]

In his whimsical way Lewis Carroll portrays time as a kind crusty individual who nevertheless can easily be offended. Making friends with him would let Alice extend her most favorite time (waiting for dinner) for as long as she liked. The unfortunate Hatter was not so lucky, however. He shook his head mournfully and explained how he once offended time (by murdering it in a musical presentation!), whereupon time had stopped at six o'clock—teatime. "It is always tea-time," said the Hatter, "and we've no time to wash the things between whiles."[3]

That was in a subterranean wonderland. Most of us find real life lived in real time to be a (sometimes uneven) mixture of good and bad times. Furthermore, we know that such times do not come empty to be filled up by us according to our will and at our discretion. The puzzling passage in Ecclesiastes 3:1-8 makes that point very clearly:

For everything there is a season, and a time for every matter under heaven:
a time to be born, and a time to die;
a time to plant, and a time to pluck up what is planted;
a time to kill, and a time to heal;
a time to break down, and a time to build up;
a time to weep, and a time to laugh;
a time to mourn, and a time to dance;
a time to cast away stones, and a time to gather stones together;
a time to embrace, and a time to refrain from embracing;
a time to seek, and a time to lose;
a time to keep, and a time to cast away;
a time to rend, and a time to sew;
a time to keep silence, and a time to speak;
a time to love, and a time to hate;
a time for war, and a time for peace.

These are the times—good times and bad times—of ordinary men and women, and they testify to our limitations before time. We are not equally successful at all times, for we meet with shifting opportunities in the world—some favorable, others unfavorable—and we cannot, like Alice, simply turn the clock to pass over adverse times; neither can we, like the Hatter, have the clock stop to remain with the good times. Instead we must take the times as they come in all their variety. That is the insight of Ecclesiastes 3:1-8.

The Problem with Time

The frustration of living within time is that we have so little control over it. Often it appears less like a friend with whom we can be on good terms. Instead we find it to be a tyrant who either rushes us through life with an inconsiderate haste or else stalls and leaves us to swelter in suffering or boredom. Can this tyranny of time be broken? Can we escape the Scylla of no time to spare and the Charybdis of too much time? Before attempting to answer these questions let us more carefully consider the twofold problem with time.

(a) *Time that will not stand still.* Firstly, we sometimes speak of time that stands still. This expression is generally reserved to describe a region, a village, or an old house that has apparently not sustained any change for a long time. We consider such places to be timeless, because here time stands still. By the same token we often define time as the measure of change we observe. For example, the time of a day involves the change from morning to evening; the time of a year is measured by changing seasons; the time of a person's life is determined by many changes from birth through old age. Even the time of a nation can be observed through changes. And it now appears possible that the time of the world itself is also measurable by subtle changes that are characterized not only by evolution but also by more troubling terms such as depletion, exhaustion, and entropy. Only when no change is observed do we say that time stands still.

Nevertheless, very few places still exist about which it can be said that time stands still. On the contrary, most places and most circumstances are changing continually, and in our generation of perennial activity things appear to be changing ever more rapidly. It is when changes occur too rapidly that we are short of time, being unable to keep up with the many changes around us. The Hatter in Lewis Carroll's story had this problem—too many teatimes. "It is always tea-time," said the Hatter, "and we've no time to wash the things between whiles." (It is ironic that this fairy tale dialogue from placid nineteenth-century provincial England should reflect so accurately the realities of many twentieth-century households—no time to wash the things between whiles). This is what we mean by saying that time refuses to stand still.

But before we get carried away in deploring the many changes that keep us busy, we must allow for the possibility that to slow up the passing of time may be neither feasible nor desirable. Perhaps the placid life of earlier generations when a man died after a long life, full of days (Job 42:17), does not offer a happy alternative to our contemporary rush. In fact, our fast living does actually provide unequaled opportunities to learn, to travel, and to do many other things that few of us would be prepared to give up. Still it does appear at least to some observers of man and his society that the speed of life has a limit beyond which living cannot reach its potential in creativity and that our time must now and again be made to stand still, so that life may become regenerated and we may be refreshed. Such times that stand still provide the step backward before the leap forward. They are not counterproductive to a creative life.

The labor legislation beginning in England in consequence of the industrial revolution, for example, was aimed at affirming the need for such times to stop once a week. It recognized that people must not be constantly engaged in work and that children especially need time to live, to play, and to grow. These early labor laws that provided time off from work once a week restored an old biblical principle of a weekly day of rest to a society that had run short of time due to pressures of production and profit. It is the thesis of this book that the ancient principle of a weekly day of rest may once again contribute to our society in the twentieth century which has also run short of time, not only due to pressures of production and profit, but also because of the fast pace of life caused by the constant changes that we have invented for our society and imposed upon ourselves.

(b) *Time that will not pass.* Before proceeding, however, a second problem regarding time calls for our brief attention. It is summed up in the frequently expressed wish that "this time will soon pass." We might expect to hear such a plea from people in distress, and it does sound from hospital beds, from people who are bent under a burden of great personal loss, who face hunger or physical displacement, and from people who as a consequence of such deprivations are unable to spend their time joyfully and creatively. But strangely enough, and this is our concern here, many otherwise healthy and well-placed people who have temporarily run out of things to do also enter this plea for time to pass. Here lies the problem of boredom—of having to fill empty time with activities so that once again it may pass.

Having to pass time that stands still can be a frightening experience to many of our contemporaries. Excess time is like a hostile environment or a dark room; we keep active, moving or whistling to cover our fear. Now consider the hard-won weekly day of rest which in our generation has grown into a long two-day weekend. What shall be done with all that empty time? Having too much time and not knowing what to do with it can be as painful as having too little time. So, in response to the prospect of a long empty weekend we have observed the development of a completely new cluster of recreational industries, all of them specifically aimed at filling empty weekends with activities. As a result we see weekend traffic rushing between suburb and sea, lake, or mountain fully equal to the weekday traffic between suburb and office or factory plant.

Nevertheless, filling empty time with such excessive and constant activity does not necessarily offer the best solution to time that will not pass. Anyone who has worked in an office or a factory is aware of the phenomenon called Monday blues. Why do people who leave off work on Friday afternoon with a sparkle in the eye return to work after a long weekend so weary and blue? Among the several reasons that could be suggested is surely one that relates to the weekend in this way: as the free time of the weekly day of rest, secured by social and humanitarian legislation, has become extended to the long weekend we now enjoy, it has been filled up with a new set of activities that send us crashing through the weekend to a blue Monday, without providing the regeneration and reconstitution that we need. In other words, responding to empty time with a spree of activities

18

is not necessarily helpful to the one who is faced with time that moves too slowly. Rather, as we have noted, it is important to learn to appreciate the value of time that moves slowly, as long as these slow moments of time are spent creatively, a matter to which we will return in much more detail. The twofold problem of time then involves facing time that will not stand still and time that will not pass in a creative way, which will enhance the quality of all our time.

Toward a Solution to the Problem of Time

We conclude, therefore, that without attempting to understand time, simply living in time can be difficult enough. First, time waits for no man. Living with time involves learning to move with time, even at the near breakneck speed with which it rushes us along. Second, time cannot be pushed. Living with time therefore also requires of us that we learn to wait for it and that we learn to "be" as well as to "do."

But how can we relate to time under these circumstances? How can we learn to move with the passing of time without succumbing to the superficiality of excessive activities? How can we make use of our free time creatively without languishing in boredom? The proposal of this book is that the old biblical concept of a weekly day of rest (sabbath) may be able to guide us into a creative use of time, both empty (free) time and full (actively engaged) time. It is well known, and not a little disconcerting, that this special day has been repeatedly abused by its proponents as well as by its critics. Some have seen in it only an arbitrary limitation to the weekly work schedule; others have found it a serious obstruction to any real pleasure after the completion of the weekly work.[4] But such repeated abuses ought not to deter our asking afresh if the fundamental idea of this special day cannot provide important insight into the life of the Christian and his time.

Finally it could perhaps be objected that it is not feasible to invoke such an old institution as the biblical day of rest in the twentieth century. To do so would not be entirely innovative, however, for history has revealed repeated attempts in past generations to invigorate the spirit of a society by invoking long-gone institutions. Bible readers are familiar with the religious and political reform of King Josiah of Jerusalem (640-609 B.C.), which began as early as 632 B.C. (II Chron. 34:1-7). However, the great and penetrating inspiration to that reform came only with the discovery of the law book (probably Deuteronomy) in the temple in the year 622 B.C. (II Kings 22:8-10). It was the contact with antiquity (the law of Moses) that set the reform under way and invigorated a generation of Jerusalemites. Incidentally, other nations in the ancient Near East (Egypt and Assyria) experienced similar attempts at spiritual rebirths during this time.[5] In more recent times the Renaissance and the Reformation were experiences of spiritual invigoration through a restoration of past institutions and ideals. The same would hold for the romantic and nationalistic movements of the nineteenth century. The history of the Christian church is dotted with such backward glances into past history in an effort to find sources of new life and vigor.

It is thus not unnatural that we should also seek new spiritual life and strength from the past, and it is certainly not strange that Christians should do so. That the biblical rest day should be the object of our backward glance is even less remarkable, for it has long beckoned us to do just that from its best-known place somewhere near the middle of the Ten Commandments: "Remember the sabbath day" (Exod. 20:8). We shall therefore remember that day in order to discover what contributions it may grant to those who live in this time—a time that alternately moves too fast, leaving us breathlessly behind, and too slowly, keeping us restless and bored.

2
Setting Time Aside

The Heritage of Our Weekend

Although our weekend is a descendant of the biblical sabbath, most people would hardly associate these two weekly institutions anymore, so scarce is our general knowledge of the sabbath. Possibly, words such as "Jew" or "synagogue" would suggest themselves in association with "sabbath," but hardly "weekend." Yet our weekend is a (perhaps wayward) child of the biblical sabbath, and it is the biblical parentage of our weekend that we seek to uncover in the hope of once again laying claim upon our spiritual heritage. To do so will require us to consider the earliest history of the Bible and the ancient customs of its people, but such an undertaking need not become very academic because the sabbath holds much of interest for anyone who counts his days in sevens.

Counting Our Days in Sevens

The sabbath is one among several special occasions of rest and festivity observed in ancient Israel, but by any standard it is the most fascinating. How did Israel arrive at this day—the seventh of each week?

In our time, most people remember years by numbers, months and days by names, while weeks are convenient measures of shorter time intervals. In ancient Israel, on the other hand, the years were numbered by the reign of the current king, while each year was circumscribed by the agricultural seasons that it provided and thus ultimately by the position of the sun in the sky. The month was determined by the phases of the moon, so that a new month coincided with the new moon, making each month twenty-nine or thirty days long. Since such lunar months are shorter than ours, something more than twelve months of this kind are required to fill up a year. Consequently, ancient Israel inserted a thirteenth month occasionally (to be exact, seven times in nineteen years) in order to fill the years completely with months and to make certain that the first month of the year would fall approximately at the same season each year.[1] Finally, the shortest calendar unit, the day, was measured in ancient Israel by its two parts, night and day. The point is that all these times of the calendar were fixed by astronomical or seasonal observations, and only later on by exact calculations based on such observations.

With the week the situation is different. It depends on no observable feature in the sky or in the fields. To be sure, attempts have been made to associate it with the moon phases that occur every seventh day or so.[2] This explanation of the seven-day week is not satisfactory, however, for observing the moon in its phases would not yield such exact intervals of seven days, especially during the last phase when the moon becomes invisible. We are therefore left with the remarkable conclusion that the weekly day of rest is simply the last day of the week. But where does the week come from?

Since most people measure the week by the names of its days, Sunday, Monday, Tuesday, and so on, we might think that the week originated as a calendar unit small enough to contain only seven named days. Furthermore, since the names of our days (Sunday, Monday, etc.) are clearly related to heavenly bodies, namely, the sun, the moon, and the planets, we might assume that the week began as a unit of seven days, one for the sun, the moon, and each of the five then-known planets.[3] Unfortunately, historical evidence cannot confirm that planetary names for the days of the week are as old as the week itself. In fact the planetary week was not known before the second century B.C., but the week is much older.[4]

What then could account for the week? Some anthropologists have found evidence that tribes in various parts of the world have held markets regularly after a certain number of days.[5] Such market days, perhaps augmented with festive or religious activities, would produce something like a week with time set aside regularly for business and perhaps other purposes. But again we have no evidence that our week began when people held market on the seventh day; in fact, the Bible denounces any market activities on the sabbath day (Amos 8:5; Neh. 13:15-22).

All this leads to the conclusion that the week is defined by the seventh day alone. But why was the seventh day chosen to close the week? The answer to this question has eluded scholarship for a long time, and a convincing answer is not yet in sight. Current thinking on the problem is focusing on the nature of the number seven. It wields a certain fascination over us, as well as over ancient Israel, and its general meaning appears to be completion or fulfillment. It is therefore not surprising that the number seven occurs frequently, also with respect to days. In fact, seven-day periods are well known, both in ancient Israel and among her neighbors.[6] Some Mesopotamian calendars name the seventh, fourteenth, nineteenth, twenty-first, and twenty-eighth days of the month as *umu lumnu* (evil day) on which certain activities of the king, the physician, and the prophet were proscribed.[7] In other Mesopotamian inscriptions, the fourteenth day of the month is named *sabattu,* that is, the day of the full moon or the second seventh day of the month.[8] All of these have a bearing on the importance of the seventh day and may contribute to our understanding of it and of its origin, but none of these provides for a continuous sequence of seven-day periods running irrespective of seasons or heavenly bodies.

The week ending in the seventh day is therefore unique, its origin is hidden in the dim past, and its persistent survival until our time is nothing short of a miracle. Such a sense of respect for the seventh day (sabbath) is intimated by the Old Testament when it affirms that the sabbath was made by the Creator himself (Gen. 2:2) and also by the New Testament when it claims that "the sabbath was made for man" (Mark 2:28). To the Christian the sabbath is a divine revelation in the truest sense. The week, then, was from ancient times a period of six days followed by a special day set aside for the purpose of concluding a segment of time. But what reasons can be found for terminating an apparently arbitrary (though unique) number of days by such a special day?

Setting Time Aside

Special days and moments that conclude a segment of time are well known to most people, though not always well understood. We may think of lunchbreaks or coffeebreaks as special moments of time that conclude hours of work. The evening and night have the same function, at least for most people, and so does the weekend. On a yearly basis we may think of such occasions as Thanksgiving, Christmas, national holidays, and summer vacation. The intervals provided by all these special times are meant to inject a certain creative quality into our ordinary times.

The Bible also knows of such special times and attributes them to the Creator himself who, according to Genesis 1:14, built such special times into his creation when he made the sun and the moon for seasons (festivals) and for days and years. Psalm 104, which is a creation hymn, illustrates this principle beautifully:

> Thou hast made the moon to mark the seasons;
>   the sun knows its time for setting.
> Thou makest darkness, and it is night,
>   when all the beasts of the forest creep forth.
> The young lions roar for their prey,
>   seeking their food from God.
> When the sun rises, they get them away
>   and lie down in their dens.
> Man goes forth to his work
>   and to labor until the evening.

—Ps. 104:19-23

Like other ancient peoples, Israel also had yearly times of rest and festivity.[9] These were determined by the agricultural seasons, but they also had deep religious significance. The Feast of Unleavened Bread in the early spring celebrated the barley harvest, but its association with the Passover made it into a commemoration of the Exodus from Egypt. The Feast of Weeks in late spring (seven weeks after Passover) was timed by the wheat harvest, but it may also have been the occasion to remember the law-giving at Sinai. The Feast of Booths in the autumn came at the conclusion of the fruit harvest, but it was also associated with the new year festival and the great day of atonement (*yom kippur*).[10]

Concerning these festivals, biblical scholarship has concluded that many of the Old Testament psalms were used in their observance, thus making these festivals extraordinary times of worship.[11] However, the Bible also intimates that they were times of festivity and joy. For example, the story of Ruth and Boaz describes how after winnowing barley (the time of the early spring festival) Boaz ate, drank, and was of a merry heart (Ruth 3:1-7). And in the otherwise unpleasant story of the Benjaminites (Judg. 19–21) we learn that the men of Benjamin seized their brides from the girls who danced at Shiloh (21:19). Since the men hid in the vineyards while waiting to fetch the dancing girls, we may assume that the celebration they planned to disturb was part of the autumn festival when the grapes had been harvested and the vineyards were no longer guarded. In short, the yearly festal occasions in ancient Israel were not only times of worship and celebration but also times of joy and festivity. This observation leads to an important principle regarding these special times and our use of them. They are not to be empty times, but must be filled with worship and celebration, festivity and joy. Our inability to generate genuine festivity, joy, celebration, and worship is, in a large measure, responsible for our failure to set aside such special times and to distinguish them from ordinary time with all its difficulties.

Special Time and Ordinary Time

Like the yearly festivals of special time, so the weekly sabbath of ancient Israel was in a unique way a day of festivity and worship, as we shall see below. But unlike the yearly festivals it has the added feature of being selected for this purpose not because of any astronomical or seasonal conditions but apparently quite arbitrarily as the seventh day. No harvest or vintage festival provides the occasion for it, no midsummer or spring rite calls for it, no darkness of winter or of night suggests its selection. It comes like an unexpected surprise, like a bouquet of flowers when there is no anniversary, birthday, or Mother's Day. This alone makes the weekly day of rest special to anyone who gives it the least bit of consideration.

In ancient Israel it began in the evening after all the work of the six previous days had been completed, at sunset time, and it lasted for one night and one day until a new week would begin.[12] The Old Testament considers it to be holy time, that is, time set apart for special purposes.[13] We will return to these below, but suffice it to say here that it is not a day of taboos, of mana, or other prohibiting qualities. Rather the fundamental purpose of this special time that is set aside is to give meaning to all time. In fact, according to the Old Testament, our relationship to this special time determines our relationship to all time. Let an illustration explain this last point.

The Mastery of Time

I receive a magazine that frequently carries advertisements for watchmakers. One watchmaker recently displayed timepieces with a guaranteed accuracy to within one second per month. This startling combination of contemporary technology (extreme precision) and ancient calendar systems (the month) cannot but fascinate anyone who is interested in the relationship between time and life; in fact, several features of this relationship crop up. One is the advancement and precision of the technology with which we surround ourselves. Another is the convenience that we enjoy. No longer do we need to wind our clocks to know the time, not to mention the inconvenience of having to listen for the chimes on city hall, the firing of cannons, the ringing of church bells, or having to watch the sun or its shadow. But thirdly, these fine watches (which measure not only seconds, minutes, and hours but also weeks and months) illustrate our need to be always on time and to adminster time with great accuracy that, paradoxically enough, has proved to be both a blessing and a curse.

Our ability to accurately measure and use time has made our activities so much more efficient. For example, executives or professional people speak of meeting so many half-hour appointments and, if necessary, of sandwiching in a few extra ones by careful timing. This can only be done by people who synchronize their activities down to the minute through a careful and precise management of time. But our use of time in this way also carries a curse, for our ability to measure and use time with great accuracy has given time an unsurpassed tyranny over us. How often have we pitted ourselves against the dispassionately and relentlessly moving arms of our watches—and lost. The clock never stops, but we do frequently and are left behind our schedule by that tiny, triumphant tick of our watch.

This tyranny of time over us can be unbearable, leaving us frustrated, angry, uptight (even with a coronary), and it is indeed a bitter mark of irony that we should use watch terminology, namely, "unwind," to indicate our only way of escape from this tyranny.

Yet "unwinding" is not an unsuitable term to characterize our relationship with the special seventh day of each week. Worship and celebration, festivity and joy, are splendid ways to unwind, providing both quiet solitude and exuberant interaction with others. On this day, given to us undeservedly and without cause, we, like ancient Israel, are again made masters of time. On this one day we can stop the watch, release the spring, unwind. Such mastery of time is less of a conquest than an understanding, however. The sabbath stands in the midst of time, between two weeks, and between two ages as well: the past and all that has been done and the future with all that might still be accomplished. It is like a traffic island in the rush of time. It enables us to get our bearing, find our direction, and plot our course. To do all that takes time, special time that will determine all other time, and the weekly day of rest is meant to provide just that.

This, then, would be the first thing to remember about the biblical heritage of our weekly day of rest as we seek from it new spiritual life and moral strength for our time: we must set time aside.

3

Time For Work

Protestant Work Ethic

"Many a father who has spent the years from 22 to 52 in a mad race to accumulate now finds himself powerless to answer his children who ask, 'Why did you do it, Pop? What did you get out of it? What have you to show for the rat race except two cars and three picture windows?' "[1]

Comments such as this one represent the reaction that many young people (and a few older ones as well) have in recent years directed against the so-called Protestant work ethic. Actually it is probably not a very satisfactory formula for explaining our material and monetary affluence. The particular "Protestant" contribution to our work ethic is surely only one, perhaps even a minor, factor in the developments that have produced such affluence. It would seem even to the casual observer of history that factors such as social structures, national spirit, availability of raw material, a capable work force, and even the strength of the stock market must be more important than Protestantism in determining the level of affluence that a nation or a society may reach.

Nevertheless, "Protestant work ethic" has become a catchy phrase to describe the character of our society. Indeed, it has almost become part of our folklore to credit it with the high level of affluence found in America and in certain other Western countries. But what is the

Protestant work ethic? Can it really claim to be Protestant? How should Christians relate to it?

Protestants and Work

The Protestant work ethic is generally traced back to the reformers Martin Luther (1483-1546) and especially John Calvin (1509-1564). The reformers' view of ordinary secular work performed by peasants, artisans, and tradesmen, as a calling or vocation approved and appointed by God, is particularly pertinent. Luther commented rather indelicately in his Genesis commentary "that man was created not for leisure but for work, even in the state of innocence. Therefore the idle sort of life, such as that of monks and nuns, deserves to be condemned."[2] His point surely is not that men and women must give themselves to unremittent hard work without leisure but that ordinary work such as tending the earth is ordained by God and is worthy of Christians. His polemic against the holy orders is characteristic but not crucial to his argument. Calvin wrote more felicitously about man's calling as a sentry post keeping him from idleness and wrong pursuits. Then he added concerning those who accept their calling, whatever it may be:

> The magistrate will discharge his function more willingly; the head of the household will confine himself to his duty; each man will bear and swallow the discomforts, vexations, weariness, and anxieties in his way of life, when he has been persuaded that the burden was laid upon him by God.[3]

It would seem only natural that such a fresh approach to work as a vocation should produce a new attitude toward work and industry of all kinds in Protestant areas. Any work (except dishonest business) was now seen as providing a suitable vocation for Christians. Calvin concluded his section on this topic in the *Institutes* as follows: "From this will arise also a singular consolation: that no task will be so sordid and base, provided you obey your calling in it, that it will not shine and be reckoned very precious in God's sight."[4] Surely, Protestantism altered our understanding of work.

Protestantism and Capitalism

It is a very long step indeed from this observation to the thesis of Max Weber. Weber, a German sociologist, proposed that Protestantism, by its attitude toward work, became responsible for the rise of capitalism with all its blessings and curses.[5] Calvinism, proposed Weber, thought of Protestantism as an asceticism of the world that can perhaps be simply explained as follows: just as a member of a religious order (a monk) would seek salvation by choosing the asceticism of his order in the cloister, so a Protestant who had found his salvation in God's justification or election would seek assurance of this salvation by choosing an asceticism of the world, that is, in work and in industry. Or put differently, as the spirit of Roman Catholicism drove its members toward the ideal of the cloister to find salvation there, so the spirit of Protestantism drove its members to the ideal of work and industry to find assurance of salvation in it.

Though this view of Weber has found supporters,[6] it has also been vigorously criticized.[7] For one thing, non-Protestants (e.g., Roman Catholics and Jews) were vitally engaged in capitalistic endeavors in the sixteenth century.[8] Furthermore, although the Calvinistic Netherlands did in fact produce an industrious and capitalistic bourgeoisie in the seventeenth and eighteenth centuries, Calvinistic Scotland showed no such tendencies. Moreover, much of Protestant Germany was as impoverished as Catholic Italy following the Reformation. In short, although Protestantism seriously altered the meaning of work, it would appear unfair to hold it solely responsible for the rise of capitalism—that aggressive "take all" spirit which will not stop short of economic domination. The reformers themselves actually vigorously opposed usury and other economic measures that would place the poor and powerless at a disadvantage.[9]

When, therefore, we speak of the Protestant work ethic, we do not necessarily describe the attitude toward work held by the Protestant reformers, but that attitude to work that developed in largely Protestant countries during subsequent centuries. Undoubtedly the reformers altered our view of work, but many other factors than the spirit of Protestantism have contributed to what we call the Protestant work ethic.

Protest Against Work

Although the Protestant work ethic may not meet with the approval of Protestantism, it has met with a great amount of protest, especially in our generation. In this sense, we may claim that the Protestant principle is at work in our Protestant work ethic![10] This Protestant principle of protest has laid open the problems of our work ethic and its assessment is well known: Work has become a religion; its faith is ambition, its rewards are wealth, its liturgy is the gentle tapping of machines, its high priest is management, and its god is progress. We are

34

committed to this religion, it has cast a strange spell over us, and we have become desperately dependent upon it.

Furthermore, this work ethic, as befits a religion, has taught us to feel guilty about idleness and leisure, as if they were sins, while anyone who defects by casting away career, wealth, or ambition is treated like an apostate, a useless parasite who no longer shoulders the burden of progress. But few have apostatized. Most are deeply committed and point with pride to what hard work has done. And indeed the technological advances in the industrialized West are impressive. Health, education, and welfare have all benefited. The ordinary comforts of life have been vastly improved. Few people would deny these benefits and fewer still would entirely forego them. Yet they have come at a cost, a cost that increasing numbers of people appear unwilling to bear.

The cost is mostly of a personal nature. The committed believer in the work ethic is often too busy to enjoy his life after work, and what is worse, to be effective, work has become largely mechanical, routine, boring, uncreative, and requiring little or no personal interest and responsibility on the part of the worker. Such work can be hellish, and it is no wonder that so many young people who are contemplating life ahead of them look at their elders and ask: "Why did you do it?" Just two cars and three picture windows cannot possibly justify such a life.

So much for the problem of our work ethic. Finding solutions to it is not so easy. To be sure, some noticeable and well-publicized attempts have been made to break the routine and boredom of so much of our work. For example, the Volvo manufacturers recently announced a pilot project in one of their car factories in Sweden. The sacrosanct assembly line would be replaced by a work bench at which a group of workers would be given the opportunity to see their work (making a luxury car) to its completion. It was felt that this approach would inject creativity back into work, instill pride in workmanship, and produce employer satisfaction.[11] Other industries have attempted to bring production and management together in planning sessions in order to instill interest in the workers toward their work, limit industrial disputes, stop assembly line sabotage, and give the worker a sense of accomplishment.[12] No doubt many more such efforts could be made with noticeable advantages, yet they may never be quite satisfactory in themselves, for much of the protest against our work ethic is directed, not simply toward uncreative, boring types of work, but toward work itself. This is so, I believe, because the apparent benefits of hard work (cars and picture windows, etc., etc.) seem so miserly, even silly, in comparison to the price we pay for them.

This, of course, is a serious misunderstanding of work and its benefits, but it is one that many Christians have not entirely escaped. Thus, when Christian spokesmen get involved in the problem of our work ethic, they often take one of two extreme positions. Either they embrace the ethic of work—hard work, prudence, frugality, and a poorly concealed affluence—as the only way to please God, or they denounce our work ethic with its rat race and materialism as an aberration of Christianity that must be corrected by radical surgery.

The Day of Rest and the Worker

We must now return to the theme of our book: the contributions of the day of rest to the life of the Christian. Can this day contribute to our relationship to work? The old commandment says: "Six days you shall labor, and do all your work; but the seventh day is a sabbath to the LORD your God; in it you shall not do any work" (Exod. 20:9-10). It is generally agreed that this commandment, though it speaks about stopping all work, is nevertheless not an injunction to work on the six days but exclusively a prohibition of all work on the seventh day. In short, we are not dealing with a double commandment: you must work on six days, and you must rest on the seventh day. It is assumed that men and women will work; the exclusive concern here is apparently to limit work to the six days.

This does not mean, of course, that the Bible as a whole lacks injunctions to work. Best known is Paul's dictum: "If any one will not work, let him not eat" (II Thess. 3:10). The Old Testament understanding of work is far broader, yet somewhat ambivalent.[13] In the first place, work is part of the Creator's basic commission to us (Gen. 1:26, 28; 2:15). According to Genesis 2:5, the earth was originally lacking in two areas: it had no water and no one to cultivate it. The mist mentioned in verse 6 could serve as a potential source of irrigation, but without the work of someone "to till it and keep it" (v. 15), no plantings would flourish. The reason for the commission to work must be sought not only in the desire to extract from the ground such products as would be needed to maintain life (see Ps. 104:14-15) by tilling it but also in the assignment to care for the earth protectively (lit., "to keep it," Gen. 2:15). Work then is an integral part of creation itself (Ps. 104:22-23). Nowhere is work understood as a curse or a burden. The work performed "in the sweat of your face" (Gen. 3:19*a*) is burdensome only because of the thorns and thistles and perhaps other adverse circumstances (v. 19*b*) under which work must now be carried out, but work as a principle of creation is not deplored.

The teachers of the Old Testament since the days of

Solomon also encouraged hard work as the only way to success and security. Some of their proverbial instructions have entered even our own language. Best known are Proverbs 6:6-11.

> Go to the ant, O sluggard;
>> consider her ways, and be wise.
>
> Without having any chief,
>> officer or ruler,
>
> she prepares her food in summer,
>> and gathers her sustenance in harvest.
>
> How long will you lie there, O sluggard?
>> When will you arise from your sleep?
>
> A little sleep, a little slumber,
>> a little folding of the hands to rest,
>
> and poverty will come upon you like a vagabond,
>> and want like an armed man.

Nevertheless, these wise teachers also present us with a feeling of ambivalence about work, and this is our second point. They question not work as such but *hubris,* that is, work which through its success deceives the worker to make it his god or his religion (Prov. 11:28; 15:16). Perhaps the most vivid warning of such deception is given in Psalm 127. In short, the Bible affirms work but not without a warning against *hubris,* that pride which pits men and women against God. It has fallen on the day of rest to mobilize that warning and send it into action in the life of the worker. Let us consider this warning by examining two references to the day of rest in the Bible.

The Day of Rest as the End of Work

Exodus illustrates the warning against *hubris* in the worker by telling a teasing story about the Israelites who gathered manna, "some more, some less" (Exod. 16:17).

Each gatherer had just enough. Any manna kept overnight bred worms and spoiled (v. 20). Apparently some Israelites exceeded the proper limits of this particular work (food gathering) by collecting extra (possibly for sale or barter) only to see it spoil. This may explain their apparent surprise over being able to gather a double amount on the sixth day (v. 22), at which point, Moses, to whom they came presumably for some explanation, was able to introduce the sabbath regulation about one day of rest in seven. Hans W. Wolff has suggested that this story is an almost humorous criticism of our restless overzealousness for work.[14] That point (don't overdo it) is also made by the worms and rot which assure that no extra manna can be kept from day to day, but it seems to me that the lesson is pressed home in a far more effective yet felicitous way by the sabbath day of rest, for on this day the commandment to stop all work is set over against God's remarkable provisions on the sixth day, as well as on all the preceeding five days. The sabbath day confirms that an adequate amount of manna has been gathered. It undercuts that human *hubris* that drives man into the field on the day of rest despite his experience with rot and worms, after he has received a clear explanation of the manna supply schedule, and although he has already secured a fully adequate supply of food. Such people "found none" is the tart and disapproving comment of the record (v. 27). Seen this way, all the sabbath laws, of which Exodus 16 contains the first (and earliest) in the Bible, may be taken as warnings against *hubris* in the worker: enough is enough!

The Day of Rest as the Goal of Work

The sabbath law that instructs the story in Exodus 16 about the manna may well have been very simple, perhaps like this: "Six days you shall do your work, but on the seventh day you shall rest" (see Exod. 23:12; 34:21). In fact, this may represent the very earliest work regulation in the Bible. It simply commands workers to do their work (lit., their doings) on six days, and to stop on the seventh. The more familiar sabbath law in the Ten Commandments is not quite so simple. The heart of it reads as follows: "Six days you shall labor, and do all your work; but the seventh day is the sabbath to the LORD your God; in it you shall not do any work" (20:9-10). Here the workers must work, labor, or serve six days by doing all their work (lit., business, task, even trade). All man's activities—whatever occupies him— must be performed during the six days, before the sabbath on which day no work is to be done.

The second of these two laws is clearly emphatic beyond the simple law with its work prohibition. However, it does seem that in this law the day of rest stands not only as an end to all work but also as a goal of all work performed on the previous six days. Its purpose is not simply to stop our activities but also to render them complete or, perhaps better, to urge their completion. Thus the day of rest represents not simply the end of all work but also its culmination and goal. This emphasis would be supported by considering the reason for the sabbath given in Exodus 20:11, namely, that God stopped his work after six days, because by then he had completed all his work and reached his goal (Gen. 2:2-3). Therefore, the rest of God reminds us that to be complete and reach its goal, work must also be creative.

Time for Work

Very busy people will often insist, and rightly so, that their time off should not be interrupted by concerns arising from their time of work. The two must be kept distinct. The proverbial full briefcase has ruined many a weekend, holiday, and even marriage. How can we keep work and rest apart? Often it is difficult, and in certain professions almost impossible. If any "workable" answer is to be found, however, a clear understanding of the biblical day of rest ought not to be neglected. It presents that special time which determines all time, even the time for work. By warning against *hubris* in the worker, it not only establishes an end for work, but it also holds up a goal for all work and thereby urges its completion. Both of these are important features of the day of rest, for it is useless to insist on bringing all work to an end, without also urging that it be completed. Unfinished work never ends. In practical terms, the day of rest appeals to the worker to set realistic goals for the week and to put forth every effort to reach these goals, thereby completing the work and bringing it to an end. Naturally, this is not always possible, for even realistic goals can be very evasive, but in such cases a concerted effort such as could reasonably be considered adequate to complete one's work will in itself become a goal reached and a task completed, whereupon all work can be set aside for rest. The day of rest, then, is a special time that determines all time, even the time for work by setting limits for it and placing goals before it. In this way it can make work creative, and surely that represents the proper ethic of work.

4

Time For Rest

Rest or Relaxation

"Work six days and get the rest free" was the theme of a meeting I once attended. Teasingly simple, but is it really true that rest follows after work, freely, as it were? Curiously, "rest" is not often used to describe that which follows work. Words such as "relaxation" or "vacation" are more common. The first of these may describe our daily after-work hours that are given to eating, watching television, and then "hitting the sack," as we say. Our weekly after-work activities may be broadened into working around the house, perhaps fishing or golf. All of these activities may be called relaxation, but scarcely rest. The holiday period following a year of work is generally taken up by travel. It is a vacation, but usually not a rest.

In fact, "rest" is a word that most people avoid, especially younger people. It carries connotations that make our health and activity-conscious society uncomfortable. We associate it with recuperation after illness, with places or activities for the elderly, with untimely or excessive sleep for the weak, or even with death. Resting, resting comfortably, resting peacefully, are all expressions associated with illness or weakness, not with the termination of work or with our response to activities.

And yet, ample evidence exists that most of us need something like rest as a response and counterpart to our work. Our very language betrays this need. Vulgar expressions such as "pooped," "had it," "beat," "worn out," and so forth describe conditions of fatigue and weariness to which rest, properly understood, is the only effective and creative response, but to say that would be to anticipate our conclusions too soon. First we must ask more precisely about this rest that is the effective and creative response to the very common experience of fatigue and weariness.

Rest and the Worker

Rest, we say, is the step backward before the leap forward. This surely represents the most elemental response of rest to work. That rest increases work effectiveness is a well-known fact that has been demonstrated statistically, notably in World War II industries. Here it was discovered that longer working hours would increase production, but only up to a point, and if the hours and days of work were increased unduly, production would actually fall over the long haul.[1] Recesses, coffeebreaks, the weekly day off, holidays, are all measures designed in a way to keep production at maximum efficiency over extended periods of time.

This is, of course, a very narrow way of viewing rest—that is, not for its own sake or for that of the worker, but solely for the sake of productivity. It is conceivable that shrewd employers may insist upon such rests, not out of the least concern for their workers, but purely from anxiety over their work. Christians would consider such an attitude questionable, if not outright immoral, because

43

they know that rest not only means to improve the effectiveness of work, it also, and more importantly, means to question our anxiety over work in a most provocative way.

Rest and Work

Popular superstition has it that worrying about one's work or responsibilities may have an adverse effect on them. The expression "leave it alone" is probably related to it. "Don't play with the paint," a master once instructed me, meaning that once the wall is painted, going over it again and again with brush or roller in over-anxiety for perfection will not improve the result. In short, sometimes the best results are achieved by leaving work alone. The parable of Jesus concerning the sower who rose day and night makes the same point (Mark 4:16-19). All the anxiety of this farmer could bring him neither understanding nor control of the growing process. "Should [he] sleep and rise night and day, and the seed should sprout and grow, he knows not how" (v. 27). Not unrelated to this parable is the frequent warning to young gardeners: Don't dig up the peas to see how they are doing once you have planted them. Some things in life are accomplished without our effort, and rest is one way of letting that happen.

This view of rest is expressed perhaps most forcefully by the Old Testament psalmist: "It is in vain that you rise up early and go late to rest, eating the bread of anxious toil; for he [God] gives to his beloved sleep" (Ps. 127:2). The context of this verse suggests that rest offers the opportunity for God to supply his friends with bread which the overzealous worker will enjoy only in trouble and without ever achieving his goals, despite long hours of work (vv. 1-2*a*).

Rest, then, responds to work in at least two very different ways. First, by providing a step backward before the leap forward, it improves the efficiency and productivity of the worker. Second, by holding off, by expressing a certain hesitancy before work, it enables work to find its own rhythm of giving and taking, which is God's rhythm. At this point, rest reveals itself in all its creative powers. On the one hand it assures men and women of the energy to embark on an aggressive "take all" course; it gives them their bustling activity and formidable strength. But, on the other hand, rest instructs workers to stop short of anxiety, to hesitate before work, to allow some things to be accomplished for them. Such rest leads workers into a pulsating experience with their world. It is a creative experience of giving and taking, in which their lives will respond to the rhythm of God, and that, of course, is an experience in time.

Rest and the World

The ecological debate has, in recent years, pointed to rest as a necessary response to the work and activities of man. Christians have inadvertently become drawn into this debate in a curious way. It all started among theologians who were anxious to demonstrate the relevance of traditional Christian theology to our contemporary scientific and technological society. They claimed that not only does science and technology owe its achievements to Christianity; these actually represent Christianity at its best. One proponent of this view was Harvey Cox in his early book, *The Secular City*. It proposed that the Hebrew understanding of creation that was passed on to Christianity separates nature from God and distinguishes sharply between nature and man. Hereby, nature becomes "disenchanted," that is, totally secular and at man's unlimited disposal, which is a prerequisite for the development of natural science.

This theory may appear to stand in Christianity's favor—as long as science and technology are considered valuable and desirable human endeavors. But with the arrival of the ecological crisis with its pollution, depletion, and many hazards to life and health, science and technology suddenly became suspect as a liability to society in the minds of many people. Then this question arose: If Christianity, thanks to the biblical teachings about God and the world, brought about the development of science and technology, is not Christianity ultimately responsible for those harmful by-products of this development: ecological breakdown, pollution, depletion, and waste?[2] How shall Christians answer this charge?

One approach would be to reassess Christianity, especially its attitude toward the world and nature. It has been suggested, for example, that the Christian ideals of Francis of Assisi would serve well as a model for our time.[3] Of special interest is the Franciscan virtue of humility in the world, its rejection of dominance, its harmony between man and animal—whether chirping birds, the fierce wolf, or the silent fish.[4] This approach would bring God and the world, humanity and nature, together again, for every creature, indeed every life, would be seen as having a soul. However, it must be asked if such a romantic relationship between man and nature is possible today. Is not the human population too large and the strain on the relationship between man and nature too severe for such rather passive idealism to succeed?

Another more promising approach would be to reexamine Christianity's fundamental understanding of the world (rather than simply its attitude toward it). Was Cox really right in asserting that Christianity and man's dominion of the world are synonomous? The key passage in the Bible is Genesis 1:26-27: "Let us make man in our image, and after our likeness; and let them have dominion over the fish of the sea, and over the birds of the air, and over the cattle, and over all the earth, and over every creeping thing that creeps upon the earth." It has been fashionable to understand man's divine "image" and "likeness" together with his "dominion" as a reference to his strength and to his autocratic rule over and free exploitation of the world.[5] But this may well be a forced interpretation of the creation story. Man's role in the world resembles that of a benevolent king far better.[6] He must not tyrannize and exploit his subjects (the world and its life) but govern them. This is also the way we must understand the expression "fill the earth and subdue it" (Gen. 1:28). The intention is that men and women must take possession of the earth and put it to proper use. Genesis 2:15 speaks of man tilling and keeping the earth. It is a matter of use, but not misuse; of tilling, but also keeping; of subduing, but not exploiting.

It seems that such an approach to the relationship between humanity and the world is more realistic than the pan-psychism of Francis of Assisi that tends to promote a passive attitude toward the world. The story of creation recognizes that the world cannot be left to its own devices; it needs a ruler to tend it, to till it, to subdue it, and to care for it. We cannot remain passive toward the world if we live in it. To believe otherwise would be naïve. "All forms of life [including man's] modify their contexts."[7] Yet how can we use and not misuse the earth, subdue but not exploit it, till it but also care for it? Or to put it differently, how can we be responsible toward the ecology?

One important answer is found in the idea of rest. The old practice of letting the fields lie fallow is a form of rest for the land. Only heavy use of fertilizer has enabled farmers to circumvent this practice in some areas but not others. Australian station (sheep farm) owners, for example, have told me that poor lands can be completely ruined through overgrazing by sheep, which have the ability to eat right down to the roots of vegetation. Unless such lands are given "rest" regularly, they become useless for a very long time. Similarly, hunting seasons are imposed so that certain desirable birds and animals may find time to rest from the hunters. These are only illustrations of what rest can do to the strained fibers in the ecological net. The world's ability to recuperate and be restored is phenomenal; even ugly scars from exploitation can mend, but that does take time.

The opportunity of nature (and society) to rest was granted the people of the Bible. The sabbatical year gave rest to the land, the jubilee year to business enterprises, and the sabbath itself to tired laborers. This principle has been called a *restitutio in integrum* (a return to the original state),[8] which implies that the world has within it energies over which man rules. These energies bind the ecological system together in a living network of interrelationships. Men and women can exploit these energies and destroy the ecology or subdue them, that is, carefully harness them into fruitful endeavors. Rest represents an important way to harness these energies, and time is a necessary ingredient of rest. But before returning to the matter of time, let us consider one more way in which rest responds to our work and activities.

Rest and Fatigue

The fatigue of our time to which rest responds is not simply physical exhaustion, such as one might experience after unaccustomed heavy work. Rather, fatigue is an experience of spiritual weariness, the combined result of fragmentation into excessive activities and of sheer boredom.[9] Many a mother has experienced such fatigue despite the many gadgets designed to make her work lighter. The endless rounds of unrelated activities bring it about: cooking, cleaning, washing, talking on the telephone, driving around, watching television, all of them easy activities, but all of them barely directed and without focus. Weariness, another term for the same experience, may describe young executives who "shuffle" papers all day long. They have many ideas and drives, but the system holds them back. So they keep up the paperwork, reports, and so forth, but they are weary of it, for they do not see its purpose or objective. Anxiety is like weariness, but applied perhaps best to the young and to the middle-aged. The young are anxious about their acceptance in a competitive and volatile society; the middle-aged are anxious about their possessions, health, position, or children. In every case fatigue, weariness, anxiety, are the result of a life without focus, a life determined by too many conflicting interests, often working at cross-purposes to each other.

Old Testament theologian Walter Brueggemann has examined this matter within the Bible and has concluded that the term "chaos" may best serve to describe the conditions of disorder that produce fatigue, weariness, and anxiety, and that rest symbolizes the only remedy.[10] The disorders in question are of the kind that leaves the world and its people in uncertainty and without direction:

a natural disaster (like the Flood), political uncertainty (when there is no king), or a military defeat (leading to the Babylonian captivity), such experiences confront the community with feelings of fatigue and weariness. Not physical exhaustion or tiredness, but an inner weariness is the result—a sense of hopelessness deriving from the fact that all one's efforts appear to be fruitless, since they have no goal or focus.

The remedy for such weariness is rest, not primarily physical rest or inactivity, but the rest that puts order into confusion and that finds a goal in disoriented activities. Biblical illustrations of this experience abound: when God established the world after the Flood he gave it rest (Gen. 8:20-22); when Israel received a king to secure her land, rest was established (I Chron. 22:9); when the Exodus delivered Israel from Egyptian slavery she was promised rest in a new land (Josh. 21:43-44); when Israel experienced her second captivity in Babylonian exile, weariness set in to replace her rest (Lam. 1:3); the Gospels speak of this rest anew in Jesus Christ (Matt. 11:28), and it is promised to the church in the end when persecutions and struggles are over (Heb. 4:9; Rev. 14:13).

Also, our own times abound with examples of the experience of weariness and rest. Psychiatrist Viktor Frankl, who spent time in a concentration camp and survived to analyze his experiences, speaks of the "existential vacuum," the feeling that life is meaningless and without direction or focus.[11] Such weariness was experienced especially by camp inmates who held no hope for a release and who could find no purpose in their experience, while those who believed in God enjoyed a much better survival record. But also many nonprisoners, says Frankl, are weary, feeling that what they do does not matter, yet they are unable to escape their meaningless-ness. Perhaps Franz Kafka's parable about the couriers expresses it well.

> They were offered the choice between becoming kings or the couriers of kings. The way children would, they all wanted to be couriers. Therefore, there are only couriers who hurry about the world, shouting to each other—since there are no kings—messages that have become meaningless. They would like to put an end to this miserable life of theirs, but they dare not because of their oaths of service.[12]

The remedy for this weariness can be symbolized by rest, a rest of order, direction, and goal. Frankl terms this remedy "logotherapy," which is the therapy of finding meaning in one's life.[13] Rest is a symbol of this meaning, the meaning that overcomes the fatigue of endless uncoordinated activities, the meaning that arrests the weariness of unfruitful work, the meaning that relaxes the anxiety that chaos will invade our carefully planned lives.

Rest and Time

Finally, how is this experience of rest related to our theme of time? According to the Bible, time is that part of the human experience that contains the meaning of life, whether we think about the former time, the right time, or the future time—our lives gain meaning and purpose-fulness from time. Said the psalmist in distress, "My times are in thy hand" (Ps. 31:15), meaning that God will put his life into order. The day of rest in the story of creation (Gen. 2:2-3) is such a time of meaning and purpose when all work has reached its goal, and all previous activities receive their focus. The rest of the Creator on this day is symbolic of the order, the purpose, and the goal of his creative activities.

Seen this way, the time of the day of rest can contribute to all our time in a number of ways. First, it brings work to its end. It is an occasion to be refreshed. It provides the step backward before the leap forward. But more than that, this day of rest answers the call to work with a response of hesitation. It allows the rhythm of give and take to pulsate throughout the whole world, so that the worker and his work may become part of a living organism. Finally, this day responds to the fatigue, weariness, and anxiety of meaninglessness. It provides a therapy of meaning through the rest which it brings. Not only are tired muscles refreshed, but also a tired mind and a tired world are given a reprieve. Restlessness is made to stop, and although spiritual weariness may stubbornly linger on, the day of rest extends an invitation to find rest even from that, and as we shall see below, it has some very concrete measures whereby that may be accomplished.

5

Time For Being Free

Freedom to Do or to Become

"He is not free who can do what he wills, but rather he who can become what he should."[1] This truth about freedom was driven home to me once during my student days in England. It happened one evening as I was waiting to enter the college chapel for the evening service. A group of foreign visitors approached the chapel, and one of them caught my attention. The dark hair and the sharp features of his face were unmistakable. It was an old friend of the family whom I had not seen for more than ten years, but I was immediately certain about his identity. So I stepped into the crowd, moved toward his side, touched his elbow ever so gently, and asked, "Mr. Seidmann, is it not?" Immediately he stepped back, stared at me nervously from head to toe, and replied in an icy voice, "No. My name is Silver." Then his story flashed through my memory as I had heard it from my mother.

Mr. Seidmann was an Estonian who had migrated to Denmark with his young wife in order to pursue his education there before World War II. He had been a classmate of my mother and later became a friend of my parents. A child was born—my age. His education completed, the family returned to Estonia. Now, for some reason that completely escapes my mind, the Soviet army at that time decided that the people of Estonia ought to transfer to Siberia, although they had lived in Estonia for centuries. Naturally, the Estonians were not in agreement with this transfer, and some of them, like our friend, knew which way to run—down through the woods, to the sea and across to Scandinavia. The women and children were crouching like animals in the forest while the men went to organize a boat, but it was too late. The cattle transport rolled in, and the family of our friend ended up in Siberia. Letters were exchanged, but to the best of my knowledge the prisoners were never returned. Meanwhile, our friend made good his escape to Scandinavia hoping for a return of his family. He was entirely free in his new land. He established a business and traveled abroad. I remember his visits to our home. He always talked about the past and how he expected one day to be found by the agents who were surely now looking for him to punish him for his earlier escape. He even changed his name to hide his true identity from the agent who would one day step up to him and ask, "Mr. Seidmann, is it not?" When, therefore, in a crowd of tourists in an unknown chapel somewhere in England, I addressed his old name with my foreign-accented English pronunciation, he saw in me that feared agent and froze up. I quickly introduced myself, and we talked about old times.

My point is that freedom is an inner quality. Our Estonian friend gained his freedom to do what he willed when he sailed into the night toward Scandinavia, but his inner freedom, his freedom to become what he should, was lost forever. Freedom, then, is not just a matter of having and doing; it has to do with being and becoming. But how can men and women become what they should? How is freedom to be found?

Freedom and the Will of God

Several hundred years ago the answer about freedom might well have been: man is free only when he renounces himself, when he gives up his own desires, and submits himself solely to the will of God (and perhaps also to the inevitable devious schemes of the devil or fate). Only by submitting to providence (or fate) can a man be free from all enslaving desires. Only by renouncing all but the will of God (the eternal order), by becoming an ascetic, can a man become what he should, namely free.

Freedom and the Will of Man

Today this medieval answer to the quest for freedom has largely been replaced by another that is concerned, not with the eternal order willed by God, but with an earthly order willed by humanity. Studies in science, economics, and psychology have shown that freedom is a fragile and evasive thing that must contend not only with the will of God but also (and perhaps even more) with conditions caused and determined by man himself. This means that freedom, which had once been sought in asceticism, came to be sought in libertinism, that is, in a maximum lack of restraints on life.[2] In other words, freedom that was once found in a submission to the eternal will of God is now being sought in conflict with the economic, political, or psychological restraints placed upon our life.

That conflict, not ascetic submission, is the new way to freedom may be illustrated by reference to Karl Marx. He insisted that the capitalistic system is not divinely ordained but that it is oppressive and will of necessity lead to conflict between labor and management. If this view is accepted, freedom can only be achieved by those who acknowledge the inevitable, namely, conflict, and participate in it.[3] Strange as it may seem to us, the original communistic ideals were in fact aimed at securing freedom for the masses (the working classes) by accepting the inevitable—class conflict.[4]

As Marx fought for freedom on the economic arena, Sigmund Freud took the battle for freedom to the inner person, who is kept in bondage by repression of the unconscious. This leads of necessity to an inner conflict between the repressive restraints (mores, convention, even religion) and the deep, liberating inner powers of men and women. Only by removing the restraints can freedom be achieved.[5]

Finally, Herbert Marcuse has attempted a synthesis of Freud and Marx by proposing that the bondage of society is not simply the work of capitalism (as Marx claimed) but is an internal bondage that the whole of our society has brought upon itself as it has been taken hostage by its own desires and inventions.[6] Consequently, freedom is not simply self-determination (in politics and on the marketplace) and self-realization (in personal life) but a total freedom involving government, economics, language, looks, feelings, and values. Our present society by virtue of its affluence as well as its poverty is not free in this sense and must be opposed by radical conflicts on a broad front. Real freedom is a freedom to be free—of both internal and external restraints and necessities; it springs from the inner man, and it will surround him with serenity.

These are the messages of some of the voices of freedom. How is freedom to be found? Is it in asceticism or in libertinism? In submission and resignation or in conflict and opposition? How can men and women become what they should?

Freedom and the Christian

Christians have wrestled with the question of freedom as much as have political economists and psychologists, for Christianity bears a message of freedom. It is a message that has often been distorted and nearly altogether lost, so much so that many people today associate Christianity with oppression and intolerance rather than with freedom. This is a matter of great embarrassment to every Christian, yet it need not rob him of his confidence in the Christian message of freedom.

Much has been said about Christian freedom. Like all forms of freedom it has traditionally been considered something one has or does, but only in part. It is much more a matter of becoming. It involves having health of body and soul as well as freedom of movement, expression, and investigation. But even more than that, it is concerned with becoming, that is, with becoming a person whose life is rich with meaning. Such Christian freedom is called by many names: truth, love, salvation, justifiation, redemption, are among them. If ever Christian freedom has failed (and the history of the church makes these failures shamefully obvious), it is not because a Christian theology of freedom has been missing or the names of truth, love, salvation, and so on have not been spoken. Rather, Christian freedom has failed when its incarnation in human experience has been missing. The suggestion of this chapter is that the day of rest provides a special time during which freedom is incarnate in the human experience.

Freedom and the Day of Rest

First of all, the day of rest, like freedom itself, is concerned with being and becoming, not with having and doing. Abstention from work on this day sets aside our preoccupation with having and doing, and its provision for worship and praise become an occasion for being and becoming. Rabbi Abraham Heschel has spoken of the weekly day of rest as an experience with time, not with things.[7] On six days, time is translated into production and possession, but on the seventh day (of rest) time is transformed into existence and eternity. This day encapsules several ideals on which freedom is nourished. Let us consider some of them.

(a) *Freedom from work.* The day of rest symbolizes freedom from work. In biblical times this was envisioned by the command to set all servants and common laborers free from their work on this day (see Exod. 20:8-11; 23:12; Deut 5:12-15). The immediate beneficiaries of this regulation would be the lower classes, foreign workers, children, and even domestic animals, and anyone else who would be around. That animals should be included would suggest that the motivation for this freedom regulation is not a purely humanitarian principle. Kindness to beasts of burden does not appear to be a natural disposition in people of the Near East. Yet, those beasts of burden are included among the recipients of this freedom, because it is based upon a more fundamental principle of harmony between master and servant, work and the worker, man and animal, and as we have already seen, between man and earth.[8] In an earlier chapter we observed how the day of rest criticizes our overzealousness for work, not because work is considered to be an evil, repressive, debilitating activity which must be opposed so that freedom can ensue. Rather the freedom of this day represents a harmony in our relationship with work: men and women must work, but their work must contribute to the larger goals of life—meaning, freedom, understanding, not just the goals of capital and profit.

(b) *Freedom from things.* The harmony that freedom gains from the day of rest must extend not only to the laborer, minors, and beasts of burden, but also to the master. In our time it is well recognized that freedom from work is needed not only by the laborer (as Marx suggested) but also and especially by the employer (Marx's bourgeoisie) and by the consumer. Today the real tyrant in our Western economy and the threat to our freedom is no longer a ruthless demand for worker performance (machines have taken that pressure off the worker); the real enemy of our freedom is our passion for production and consumption. It is the benefits rather than the costs of work that take away our freedom. This is too well known to require much elaboration, but it is reasonably obvious that the clothing industry, the cosmetic industry, the automobile industry, and so on, would all like to persuade the consumers that they cannot make do without their latest products. Advertisers do not grant the consumers the freedom to value an older product, or no product at all in place of a new product, and most consumers appear to have quite helplessly parted with this freedom. It is the benefits rather than the hardships of work that rob us of our freedom today.

In this complex situation the weekly day of rest is a day of freedom in every way. To those who bear the burdens of labor it offers a reprieve, a day of freedom from work; to those who bear the burdens of profit and consumption, it demands a reprieve. To the former it gives freedom; from the latter it exacts it. On this day, the rich do not get richer and the poor do not become poorer. On this day, the university professor and his freshman student who just failed three classes may share the same pew in chapel—there is neither pressure nor obligation to be exerted. On this day, the business executive and his janitor share the same national park or beach, and no one gives the other an order or extracts a service. No one may take advantage of the other. In short, the freedom that this day inspires is not partial or provincial or paternal. It is not graciously extended by the upper classes, nor is it violently and belligerently extracted by the working classes from big business. Rather it is a freedom that penetrates all levels of society, and it is not secured by some at the expense of others.

(c) *Freedom and equality.* These qualities of freedom inspired by the day of rest leads to another important observation: freedom implies genuine equality. In Bible times equality was an important part of religious activities. Before God all were equal—young and old, slave and free, man and woman (I Sam. 1:3-8). Religious activities were all quite innocent; even children were welcome to participate (Deut. 6:20-25); all were equal. Freedom and equality belong together in times of worship, and this equality is genuine, meaning that it breaks down the barriers between people without denying the obvious differences between them. It does not pretend that such differences do not exist. Few attitudes are more offensive in human relationships than pretended equality. Biblical religion makes different classes of people equal before God and therefore before each other. That is genuine equality.

A religious inscription from Lagash in ancient Mesopotamia (third millenium B.C.) explains this equality on a religious day in a movingly simple way: "In the days in which the king (Gudea) entered the house, in seven days, the maidservant made herself equal to her mistress, the manservant walked beside the master."[9] The Bible itself contains no exact parallel to this regulation, but it does imply that the freedom on the day of rest brings equality into society. Deuteronomy 5:14 instructs that on the day of rest the laborer must be set free so that like his employer he too may rest. The related institution of the sabbatical (seventh) year presses this home even more effectively. Exodus 21:1-6 requires a slave to be given the option of freedom on the sixth year of his slavery, but even such an opportunity may not provide complete freedom, for the master who has freed his slave may still view him as just a freed slave, not as a liberated man. Deuteronomy 15:12-18 therefore expands the same law of freedom by adding the instruction that a freed slave must be given generous gifts—enough to make him independent of his liberator. Only then is freedom complete—when it becomes independent of the one who bestows it.

(d) *Freedom and harmony.* By its very nature, Christian freedom, inspired and instructed by the day of rest, becomes not just freedom "from" but also freedom "for." Freedom "from" would be freedom from various repressive tyrants such as greed, possessions, masters, or customs. Such freedom can be achieved by overthrowing (sometimes violently) these tyrants. It enables us to do what we want. That is the freedom of Marx and Freud, and of some Christians as well. But true Christian freedom is rather a freedom "for." Hans Küng has illustrated this freedom by meditation on the life of Sir Thomas More.[10] More was a man of wealth who enjoyed his possessions and did not seek to be rid of them (though he was always generous), but neither was he deeply

61

attached to them. He attained great power and wielded it with skill and authority, but he was always free to relinquish it. He was endowed with a brilliant intellect and made good use of it, but he possessed a fine sense of humor and could laugh at himself. He was devoted to his family, but not overindulgent, and so on.

Such a harmony or balance in the experience of Christian freedom is the contribution of the day of rest. It does not denounce work, production, or even consumption, but it urges that we put a distance between us and these potentially repressive tyrants—not so wide a distance that we are bound in isolation or so near a proximity that we are bound in unbreakable attachment. On this day work is stopped because it is completed, yet work is not denounced. Workers are set free, but they are not sent away; instead they enjoy equality with all members of the community. Consumption does not cease entirely, for life must go on even on the day of rest, but all overdulgence is abandoned. On the day of rest we are not only free from our masters of work, possessions, desires; we stand free before them. Whether it is work or greed or mastery or consumption that threaten us, the day of rest, if we take it seriously, sets us free before these. It does not rob us of the things of our life, but it takes away their dominion over us on this one day. Such is the freedom of the day of rest. It is granted to the individual but extends to all of society. It is offered in the time of one day each week, but it beckons us to extend the blessings of this special time to all time. Then we shall be free, indeed.

6
Time For Recreation

Time that Recreates

The late Rabbi Abraham Heschel, who during his tenure at the Jewish Theological Seminary in New York became a friend of many people, once wrote this about the day of rest: "We usually think that the earth is our mother, that time is money and profit our mate. The seventh day is a reminder that God is our father, that time is life and the spirit our mate."[1]

In this chapter we shall explore still another contribution of the day of rest to our ordinary time, namely the contribution of recreation, not just physical recreation (we will return to that in a later chapter), but rather recreation of the inner person and of life itself. But first some definitions.

Recreation, Leisure, Entertainment, and Rest

Recreation will be taken in its literal sense as re-creation. As such, it differs from both leisure and entertainment. The latter involves experiences undertaken for their own sake—although they may, of course, also contribute to a balanced life in a general way. However, leisure and entertainment are not primarily designed to contribute to the rest of our life; they are an end in themselves. Recreation, on the other hand, though it may be very enjoyable in itself, nevertheless has always an ulterior motive, namely to contribute to the rest of life. Often enough leisure is also recreational, and that may be true even of entertainment, but recreation is never self-contained; it always looks to all of life.

Recreation also differs from rest, which implies stopping work and activities, for it is generally active. However, it involves activities that do not, like work, drain our energies, but restore them.

It is not easy to provide adequate illustrations of the difference between these terms, but activities such as hiking, surfing, pursuing a hobby, or attending a party may be considered recreational. A cruise, a drive, or a visit to one of our many popular resorts could be termed leisure, while watching a show or a movie could be termed entertaining. All of these *may* contribute to our ordinary life, but recreation *insists* on doing just that, while rest is a release from the pressure of life.

Feast and Play

So our question is, how can re-creational activities influence, even transform everyday life? At this point we may consider the recent interest in the function of play and feast in our society. This interest probably has arisen out of a popular reaction to the brave new world of science and technology in which God was reduced to an event in politics or history.[2] But now we have lost our courage. Life in the "technopolis" has become frightening for very real reasons: the threats of technology gone amuck, the fears and loneliness among depersonalized people, and the emptiness of life without a center—these have made our brave new world almost unbearable. We need to find meaning in our technology, mystery in our science, joy in our "technopolis," but how? The answer is feast and play. Feast refers to an experience that enables us to extend our awareness of life and its meaning to the full. Feast overcomes the threats of technology by removing our dependence upon it, it eases the fear and isolation among people by providing communion and fellowship, and it brings into the present both our past heritage and our future hope. Feast brings meaning into our lives and renews them. In this sense, feast is re-creative. But what is the experience of feast in practice and how can it occur?

David Dancing Before the Ark

One well-known biblical illustration of feast is David dancing before the ark.

> And David danced before the LORD with all his might; and David was girded with a linen ephod. So David and all the house of Israel brought up the ark of the LORD with shouting, and with the sound of the horn. (II Sam. 6:14-15)

The occasion for this exuberance was David's obvious success as king of Jerusalem. He had taken the city of the Jebusites (former Canaanite inhabitants of Jerusalem) with great imagination, courage, and success (5:8-16). Prior to that, he succeeded in earning the loyalty of the northern ten tribes (v. 1), although he had defeated their king. Their common enemy, the Philistines, had been decidedly defeated (vv. 17-25). Thus, the kingdom was united, secure, and established. Everything had turned out well. Past promises of blessings had caught up with David, and his hopes for the future were unfolding daily before his eyes. This day the ark (a symbol of God's presence) was coming into Jerusalem to confirm it all. This day, past promises and future hopes converged in one event, and that is feast.

King David was a master of feast, not only in favorable times, but also at unfavorable time, as in the case of his child's death. It was the child Bathsheba conceived in the illicit affair on David's roof while her husband Uriah was overseas fighting David's wars (II Sam. 11). A very shameful affair. The child was born but immediately took ill ("the LORD struck the child," 12:15*b*), and David mourned—so deeply that his servants feared to break the news of the child's death. Then David saw them whisper, guessed what had happened, and proceeded to shock his servants by washing, dressing, and annointing himself (as for a party). He visited the temple to worship and returned to his palace for a meal, but why? His answer is instructive: "While the child was still alive, I fasted and wept; for I said, 'Who knows whether the LORD will be gracious to me, that the child may live?' But now he is dead; why should I fast? Can I bring him back again?" (vv. 22-23). It is by simple, yet marked, activities of fast and feast that the experience of a dying child is integrated into ordinary ongoing life so as to enrich and enlarge our perception of it.

In this, Michal, his first wife, differed from David. She was offended by his dancing before the ark; she expressed it and told David so: "How the king of Israel honored himself today, uncovering himself today before the eyes of his servants' maids, as one of the vulgar fellows shamelessly uncovers himself" (II Sam. 6:20). For Michal, David's dance was an irresponsible act of play that would only bring confusion and chaos: a king must not let go of himself in this way. Michal is a practical realist who knows what is right; she will not let go of herself for fear of losing face; she positions herself "into the windowframe of a narrow morality";[3] she looks down upon David from her position of orderly safety; she will take no risks. From this reserved position in her window she did no wrong, but by refusing to share in the joy of her king, she missed an important part of life—namely, that joyful ecstacy of life and of freedom and of God that converged on this day in Jerusalem. "And Michal the daughter of Saul had no child to the day of her death" (v. 23).

King David was less cautious, and he shocked some members of his court, but in his dancing and feasting he was able to touch the very nerve of life. That is the meaning of feast. The Bible offers a few other references to this symbolism of play and joy at crucial instances. Job 38:7 describes the founding of the earth when "the morning stars sang together and all the sons of God shouted for joy." Wisdom is represented as being (playfully) beside the Creator when the world was made (Prov. 8:30). And in Zechariah 8:5, boys and girls will again be playing in the streets of Jerusalem when God returns to Zion. Some of the illustrations point out that play can be both dramatic and violent. Samson plays (makes sport) before the lords of the Philistines when he brings the roof down upon them (Judg. 16:25), and when the young men of Abner and Joab play by the pool at Gibeon the hatred of two national factions realizes itself in deadly violence (II Sam. 2:14-17). The point is that these experiences of play summarize the reality of life in an unmistakably clear and dramatic way, and conversely, it is through play, feast, and celebration that everyday life is charged with the dynamic energy which is of the essence of life.

Festive Time and Ordinary Time

We must now turn to the experience of feast in our time. In doing so we must consider two questions: (a) What is the relationship between feast and everyday life? (b) How does the special time of the day of rest contribute to our experience of feast? But first, let us examine the relationship between feast and everyday life. What possibilities do feast, play, and joy have of being truly re-creational?

(a) *Feast that accepts life.* According to one view, feast teaches us that all of life is a play, and its contribution to our experience of life is to make it playful.[4] To live means to become a child who enjoys what he does and savors every moment of it, but not so much that he cannot stop his game. Here is no distinction between the serious and the nonserious. We do our work in a detached sort of way, but joyfully, and we relate to others playfully and with a minimum of obligations. We find joy in everything and so we approve of everything.[5] But can our life really be re-created in such a playful, all-approving, uncritical way? Would not such a feast, such re-creation, be doomed to failure because it has failed to meet the ethical responsibilities of facing "the great dragon" of oppression and responsibility?[6] Or, as Grammer Gurton asks of those "playboys" who wish to make every day a feast, "Who is the cook?"[7] In other words, feast that sets out to simply and uncritically make life playful fails to take account of the pain, grief, and responsibility of which life is so full.

(b) *Feast that rejects life.* According to a second view, feast re-creates life, not by affirming it or approving of it, but by totally opposing it. Here feast relishes in excess; it throws off all restraints, like a carnival. In the carnival propriety is set aside, and duties and responsibilities are rejected or forgotten. Make-believe has taken the place of reality, which is hidden behind masks. Protected by masks, we are free to do what we do not ordinarily dare and to imagine that we are what ordinarily we could never become. Behind masks we do not approve of, but reject real life. But does such festive opposition to and rejection of ordinary life really offer a re-creation of life? It cannot! For to be truly re-creative, feast must neither fully affirm ordinary life by pretending that it is all a play nor fully deny it by opposing and ignoring it in excessive abandon. There is a middle way whereby feast shares in joyful abandon but does not reject its responsibility toward life. It is at this crossroad that true recreation takes place, and there life is enlarged and renewed in meaning in unexpected ways. But how do we arrive at this crossroad?

Day of Rest and Feast

This question takes us to the weekly day of rest that in a unique way embodies the type of feast which is re-creative. Understood as such a feast, the day of rest will emerge as special time that can enlarge and enhance the quality of all time. To this matter we will now turn.

(a) *Day of rest as festive non-doing.* First, the day of rest is a daring "non-doing."[8] The tone is set already in Genesis 2:1-3. On the seventh day the Creator dares to drop his creative work. Of course, he had finished his work before he stopped it, but is a creator ever finished with his work? Is not the challenge before a creator a challenge to stop? Is there not a triumphant note of daring in this stopping, as when an artisan has just completed a piece of complicated machinery and then, withdrawing his clamps and tools, dares it to work? This daring to stop on the seventh day recurs in the story of the manna supply that came in equal portions on five days; then a double portion followed on the sixth day with none on the seventh (Exod. 16). The question is, Will the people attempt to gather manna on the day of rest, or dare they depend on leftovers from the previous day, although ordinarily leftovers would spoil in just one day? Many apparently dared, but some did not (v. 27). The day of rest stands spitefully before the weekdays of work. Its rejection of work is excessive and dramatic, as the Old Testament sabbath laws make clear: "Whoever does any work on it [the sabbath], that soul shall be cut off from among his people" (31:14). Is it possible that a law such as this one should be read by us not simply as a strict prohibition of work but as a daring invitation to cast off all work—a reckless abandon in free time and a daring demonstration against the necessity of the daily routine. The businessman closes his attaché case, the contractor lets the telephone ring, the housekeeper allows the washing to wait, and the student closes his books.

That the sabbath laws should be understood this way is further suggested by the festive quality of the day of rest. It was a day of worship (II Kings 4:23; 11:4-12; I Chron. 23:30; Isa. 1:13; Hos. 2:11). One psalm, which is specifically assigned (in intertestamental times) to the sabbath worship, is a hymn of thanksgiving, sung in a festive mood with musical instruments (Ps. 92:3).

It is this festive and worshipful quality of the sabbath that has enabled it to transform strict prohibitions of work into a freedom from work, and thus room has been made for the experience of joy and even play in the lives of men and women. Such joy and play is the "work" of children whereby they participate in the real (!) world of adults by imitating it. But also adults need play. In their play the shackled human spirit is released from its toil and conflicts so that it may rise to a new experience of life. Play sets the imagination aflame, it opens new possibilities to challenge present impossibilities, it invites abandon but not escape. Humor that accompanies good play may contribute to the same experience.[9] Of course, play must not be confused with reality; the two are distinct and stand over against each other, but they contribute to each other. Yet many people no longer know how to celebrate, to play, or to laugh. Idleness is often associated with sin, and recreation is subject to considerations of profit and advantage. Even our festivities are sometimes carried out with a vengeance that have robbed them of much of their joy and playfulness.

These two qualities, a daring "nondoing" and a festive playfulness are combined in the day of rest. Together they enable this day to transcend the world of labor, servitude, and conflict of interests, and to provide imaginative insights into the world beyond—the world of God. Sabbath observers sometimes imagine that on this day the trees and mountains are more beautiful than on any other day or that the weather is better on this day than on all others or that dinner tastes better than ordinarily. Such imaginative play is a spiritual exercise, the activity of spiritual children whereby they transcend the things of this world and experience in some way the things of God's world. This spiritual playfulness of the day of rest can penetrate into every day, for the day of rest is that special time that completes and fulfills all time. On this day the week with its work is finished, and it now appears for what it must be—creative time whose work is carried out with playful and joyful imagination.

(b) *Day of rest as responsible doing.* At this point a second consideration arises as we examine the contribution of the special time (the day of rest) to all our time. Not only does the day of rest challenge our week of work by making it joyful, playful, and re-creative; it also constantly questions the value of our works. It asks if our works are good. The day of rest provides no sense of completion and fulfillment when our works are evil or unfinished. It does not simply neutralize our work with joy and play; it invites our work to be completed and fulfilled in joy, in play, and in creativity.

The prophet Isaiah hints at this affirmation of work on the day of rest. Isaiah 1:13, for example, contains a condemnation of sabbath observance practiced in the eighth-century B.C. Jerusalem temple because at this time people were combining the sabbath festival with iniquity (evil works). That is an impossible combination, for the sabbath cannot fulfill such works; it questions them and judges them. In Isaiah 58:13-14 that point is driven home forcefully.

> If you cease to tread the sabbath underfoot, and keep my holy days from your own affairs, if you call the sabbath a day of joy and the LORD's holy day a day to be honored, if you honour it by not plying your trade, not seeking your own interest or attending to your own affairs then you shall find your joy in the LORD. (NEB)

The sabbath, says the prophet, is not the time to seek one's own advantage; it is the day to find delight in God.

Unfortunately, many sabbath observers have interpreted this as an invitation to enforce strict sabbath regulations prohibiting all work on this day, although the contexts of this verse (Isa. 58:1-12) makes it quite clear that the one who finds delight in God is the one whose works have been good, who can look back on a week in which bonds of wickedness have been loosed, hungry mouths have been filled, and naked bodies have been sheltered (vv. 6-8).

The joy and playfulness of the day of rest are not the results of being finished with such mundane and unpleasantly trivial duties (for that would only bring quarrel and fighting, v. 4); they appear rather when such duties are carried out creatively and have been completed. Luke's Gospel tells a beautiful story that illustrates this very point. A woman had carried a burden of illness for eighteen years (Luke 13:10-17). Jesus promptly removed that burden of illness by healing her, but the ruler of the synagogue was critical: "There are six days on which work ought to be done; come on those days and be healed, and not on the sabbath day" (v. 14). Jesus' reply is well known: even an ox or ass receives special consideration when in need on the sabbath, how much more this woman whose burden has not been lifted for eighteen years, and how appropriate that the sabbath should provide the occasion for this work to be fulfilled.

The day of rest then has the capacity to do two things: it can ask critically about our works, and it can respond to our finished works with joy and playfulness. This makes it re-creative. But is there a practical side to it all? I believe so. The day of rest sets goals before us, duties to be carried out, jobs to be finished, meals to be prepared. It fills our days with work. It does not promise us a utopian world inhabited by "play people." But it does set goals before our work, and it dares us to realize these in a special time of no work. That is a time of play and joy, alone or with others, in playful luxury or in austere joy. Walking, sailing, riding, talking, listening, seeing, hearing—all the things that fill us with joy belong on this day. By our play and joy we realize that our work has indeed been finished and completed. In its turn that completed work contributes to our joy and play and calls for more in the time ahead. The day of rest has become a time of re-creation because it recreates and enables us to create anew.

7

Time For Worship

Worship Is a Response

"Worship," says Walter J. Harrelson, "is an ordered response to the appearance of the Holy in the life of individuals and groups."[1] Two things need to be added to this definition of worship before we proceed. First, that worship has once again in our time emerged as an important part of our experience. It was argued in recent years, even by Christians, that worship can find no meaningful place in our secular age. That argument began with Dietrich Bonhoeffer's suggestion during World War II that Christianity has finally become "religionless." Now in a religionless (secular) Christianity, worship would certainly be conspicuous by its absence, for worship more than anything else has long provided definitive proof that Christianity is a religion, and that naturally bothered Bonhoeffer, as it would any thoughtful Christian. Worship, after all, is not a demonstration of holiness (religion), but a response to holiness, as Harrelson so aptly points out. Still worship—that religious side of Christianity—has not vanished as readily as Bonhoeffer predicted in the now-famous letters written during his prison term. To be sure, many traditional forms of worship have all but vanished or are seriously strained, but worship itself has simply reemerged in new forms, perhaps less structured than before but nevertheless very real. The charismatic movement, for example, is largely a form of worship. The new awareness of the supernatural, whether as occultism in its most grotesque form or as fundamentalism in certain church denominations or as piety in civil religion, is also a form of worship.[2] It would seem, therefore, that worship is very much going to stay with us. Perhaps that is inevitable, for worship represents man's response to the appearance of the holy, and man, as we sometimes say, is "hopelessly religious,"[3] that is, he lives in the presence of the holy. Only with great effort can he cut himself loose from its presence, and then just temporarily.

The second thing to be observed is that worship is an ordered response to the appearance of the holy in the life of individuals and groups. If disordered, the response is not genuine worship. Instead it may be a response of terror, confusion, or even anger, and it may become destructive to life. An ordered response in worship, on the other hand, affirms and sustains life. We have ample illustrations of disordered responses to the holy. Bizarre and highly emotionally intense experiences with the occult, perhaps exorcism, are in my view disordered responses to the holy, for they invoke fright, threats to life, and perhaps even mental imbalance bordering upon insanity.[4] At the other extreme lie those responses that are characterized by the lethargic ease and carefree abandon in some religious communes whose ideal is to be natural, to be moved rather than to move, to be carried by the spirit rather than to invoke it. Some of these responses I find equally disordered, for they assume a rhythm and a harmony in life that do not correspond to common human experience. To let such a rhythm of life (joy and sorrow, birth and death, play and work) guide our response to the holy is no guarantee of orderliness, for the rhythm of life can be perplexing. Birth does not always follow a natural and harmonious rhythm of love, conception, and joyful expectation; death is seldom a harmonious acceptance of a fulfilled life; and as behavioral science has taught us, even joy and sorrow are most unpredictable and at times unmanageable experiences.

Worship and Holiness

What, then, is the ordering principle in our response to the appearance of the holy? How shall we worship? The ordering that biblical worship brings to life is primarily an ordering of time. This point, says Harrelson, has been greatly overstressed in recent literature.[5] Still it does represent a crucial insight into the meaning of biblical worship, and it is very nearly right. The physical world—mountains, springs, trees, new births, the holy fire on the altar, the priest in his holy robes, the king in his splendor—all these may represent manifestations of the holy, and worship responds to these with praise, joy, or fear. This is not denied. Nevertheless, it is when holiness enters time that our response in worship becomes incisive, and it is the ordered response to holy time that has profoundly contributed to our Christian experience of worship. Therefore, a most important ordering principle in our response to the holy is time, and the most important such time of biblical worship is the day of rest. We can now ask the two basic questions that will occupy our attention for the remainder of this chapter: First, what is the importance of letting time be the occasion for the holy to appear and thus for worship? And second, what contributions can the time of worship make to all our time?

The Appearance of the Holy

(a) *Holy places.* In one of his talks upon the sabbath, Rabbi Heschel contemplated his view of Arizona and Nevada from an aircraft flying west. Such vast (for an Easterner), empty areas lay beneath: rocks, forests, deserts, streams, space. All part of God's good earth, provided for our delight and use. Nowhere, commented Rabbi Heschel, nowhere in sight was any holy mountain or sacred grove or spring. No place, no object, was made holy by the Creator. All God's good earth is secular, which means that it belongs to the realm of the world. Thus, it came from the Creator's hand. Only time was sanctified with these words: "So God blessed the seventh day and hallowed (sanctified) it, because on it God rested from all his work which he had done in creation" (Gen. 2:3). Time, not space, is primarily imbued with holiness. Therefore, time rather than space (places, objects, individuals) calls for a clear response in worship.[6]

Of course, Rabbi Heschel was overstating his case with characteristic disarming charisma. Had he flown over the vast empty interior of Australia, another continent the size of our own, he might have observed Ayers Rock below, huge and mysterious, looming eerily over the horizon. It is a sacred rock that has drawn aboriginals to its caves since the dawn of time. Even today it draws its admirers who in fascination record its changing moods and colors on film. Truly an exceptional place. So are the springs at Baniyas in northern Israel where below the rock face the waters of Jordan emerge from the interior of the earth. Also, our own land holds many such places that draw us near for reasons we can hardly explain. Is it their beauty or the lore that grew up around them or the pull they exert upon our soul? In any case, we too have our places of worship, some in nature, others of human origin. They draw us, captivate our imagination, and can profoundly influence our lives.

(b) *Holy times.* Yet, Rabbi Heschel was right about the role of time in biblical worship. That time alone of all God's creations should be sanctified in the face of such a vast expanse and variety of space must not escape our notice. Perhaps we could continue Rabbi Heschel's fantasy by asking further about God's creation. What would have happened, we might ask, if God had not stopped his creative work on the day of rest to sanctify it with his presence? Would he have expanded his space further? Would he have spun new galaxies in distant parts of his universe? Would he have flung handfuls of stars about? Or lighted new suns in dark corners of his realm? Would he have formed great mountains, planted more trees, or modeled new people like himself? And what then would have been the fate of men and women—his choice creation? Would they not have moved from place to place, from mountain to spring, from tree to rock, from sun to moon, always moving on, working, doing, planning? At no time would they rest at any place to savor its meaning and to feel its presence. All things would pass by them swiftly, like flying over vast spaces.

But holiness in time is not so. It refers to a special quality of the day of rest, a time when God rests and lets himself be found, and that is when holiness appears. Consequently, if worship is our response to the appearance of the holy it too must occur in time, and the most important worship time is that provided by the day of rest. Rest is what makes the seventh day a time of worship, for it is in resting (stopping) that the holy finds occasion to appear. H. H. Rowley once wrote: "It is

79

significant that in our day impatience with the sabbath as a day of rest is the accompaniment of the widespread abandonment of the sabbath as a day of worship."[7] His point is that the day of rest offers an occasion for worship even in the absence of temples and that holy time cannot be lost to material destructions or even exile; it only succumbs to preoccupations with work and with the things of this world.

This understanding of worship has received prominence in the Bible, even where we least expect it, namely at the occasions when temples were established. King Solomon asked at the inauguration of his temple: "The LORD has set the sun in the heavens, but has said that he would dwell in thick darkness. I have built thee an exalted house, a place for thee to dwell in for ever. . . . But will God indeed dwell on the earth? Behold, heaven and the highest heaven cannot contain thee; how much less this house which I have built!" (I Kings 8:12-13, 27). And about later temple worship the prophet asks: "Heaven is my throne and the earth my footstool; what is the house which you would build for me, and what is the place of my rest?" (Isa. 66:1).

(c) *Holy day of rest.* It seems to me, however, that the day of rest is not an important occasion for worship simply due to such a pragmatic consideration, namely, that when our holy places are lost we can always resort to holy time. Rather the value of holy time is fundamental. Time represents the foremost medium of holiness in the Christian experience, at least as the Bible sees it. We do admit that a person, an object, or a place may witness the appearance of the holy; Christians may indeed see a priest, touch a cross, or visit a shrine where the holy may appear, but only at the right moment, and that is the moment when all other preoccupations are set aside. The day of rest is such a moment that sets aside all preoccupations in favor of the one that responds to the holy. The day of rest is not a special time that can conjure up holiness. It contains no magic, uncanny powers. It is the setting aside of all other preoccupations (rest) that sanctifies this day. Holiness cannot be demanded from a priest or extracted from a place or controlled in an object. Holiness can only be experienced by providing it with the occasion, which is setting aside all other preoccupations. In this sense, Rowley is quite right in claiming that impatience with the sabbath as a day of rest leads to its abandonment as a day of worship, for worship is a response to the holy, and the day of rest is time which provides it with the occasion to appear. When we find no time for the holy, moss grows upon our altars. Without time, holiness is mute and worship ceases.

In the Bible the day of rest is seen as a prominent occasion for the holy to appear and for worship to result. It is not the only such occasion, but it is an important one, not least because it occurs regularly every seventh day. Some have pointed quite correctly to the regularity and predictability of this day suggesting that these features have blunted its holiness. But a more important aspect of its regularity is its persistence. It will cut short our secular preoccupations with uncompromising regularity; it will not delay; it will not let holiness be lost. To some, this regular invitation to worship is a burden, but to others it is a distinct blessing, for it assures that an experience of the holy is never far from the one who seeks it and wishes to respond to it. No pilgrimage to distant sacred sites is required, no penance must be paid, no burden must be carried. Holiness and the invitation to worship come quietly and unobtrusively once each week—whenever time is set aside—to everyone who stops and rests and provides it with the occasion. What, then, is the contribution of the day of rest to worship? It provides time for the holy to appear and makes worship possible. This takes us to our second question.

Responding to Holiness in Time

We began by noting that "worship is an ordered response to the appearance of the Holy in the life of individuals and groups," and we must now direct our attention to this "life" mentioned in our definition by exploring further the worship that we experience in time: what is its nature, and how does it contribute to the life of the Christian?

Worship on the day of rest, we have found, is an ordered response to the appearance of the holy in time. The response is ordered because it orders. In other words, by ordered we do not mean simply "order of worship," though this may, of course, be involved. Rather, we must think of that aspect of worship which orders. From this it follows that worship which responds to the appearance of the holy in time represents an ordering of our time. This can happen in several ways.

(a) *Our past.* First, there is past time. For many people the past time is an "unholy mess," a jumble of experiences that sends conflicting impulses into the present. Past failures bring lingering fear and discouragement, even disgust. Why did I ever do that? we keep on asking ourselves a long time after. Past stupidity stays with us stubbornly—forever, so it seems. But the past also brings out some success for our recollection—at least in the case of most people—glorious moments of happiness when the future looked bright or proud moments of success when we reaped compliments that really counted. Why can we not repeat those moments, relive them, conjure them up, and bring them back to life? So often they are just like ghosts—somewhere in the distance, but not really real. Such is our past. It comes to us as a sorry mixture of failure and success and confronts us with a disorder of threats and hopes.

Worship sets out to bring order into these past experiences as it responds to the appearance of the holy in the present. Its response is one of forgetting and remembering. Paul once referred to this response in a different context: "One thing I do, forgetting what lies behind and straining forward to what lies ahead" (Phil. 3:13). Years later theologian Paul Tillich asked in a sermon on this text, "What did Paul forget?"[8] Clearly, he wished to forget his unhappy past life as a Pharisee and a persecutor of Christians, but every letter he wrote demonstrates that he never forgot. This forgetting then is not a simply psychological experience of losing the past in the way we lose our activities and thoughts of, for example, last Monday, nor does it involve repressing past experiences which are too painful. Rather it is a forgetting that remembers; it is a forgetting of forgiveness, of being released from the past, of being liberated from its failures and pain, of being free to remember all of this painful past and yet to see in it an ordered life. That is the task of worship. It looks back and puts the past in order, not by denying it or suppressing it, but by facing it freely and by integrating it into our life. This is the first response of worship to the appearance of the holy in time: it orders our past.

(b) *Our present.* Second, there is our present experience. Does worship also bring order to the present time? The present does not really exist as a separate time, for time does not ever stand still.[9] The present is but the experience of seeing the future slipping into the past. That happens continuously. The future is thrust upon us; it flings open the present and moves into the past. We cannot stop this process or delay it much; we must respond to it. It is not a matter for us to determine our future, but to determine, if possible, the kind of past it will become once it has passed us. The task of the present is to make the future into our kind of past. The present therefore, is composed of a series of decisions.

Worship cannot do away with those decisions, but it can assist us in making them. First, it has set us free of the past and of those shameful deeds that give us complexes and make decisions so difficult. Our response to the appearance of the holy in the present will therefore be fresh and new and open. It remembers all the possibilities and failures of the past, but stands forgiven before them and released from their handicaps. Past experiences of overconfidence no longer clamor for repetition, and past failures do not stymie our courage. The present is ordered by worship's response to the holy in time: it is free to face the future.

(c) *Our future.* Finally, the future is the most mysterious and confusing part of our time. History is full of attempts to bring order into the future—most of them unsuccessful. Mighty men and women of all ages have attempted to control the future by eliminating some and anticipating other of future's possibilities, but a few were always left unattended. Meanwhile, the future keeps coming at us. Stopping it is like stemming the flow of a stream with a dike. Many wise men and women have attempted to master the future by seeking to know it in advance or guessing it, but it nearly always springs surprises to warn us that the future is ultimately unknown. We must therefore face the future anew constantly; it comes upon us in all its confusing variety and sometimes nearly overwhelms us with its unpredictable mixture of potential happiness, joy, frustration, anger, possibilities, reverses, and plain enigmas. How can we bring order to this confusing assault of time?

Worship in time does not predict the future. Holiness comes into our lives not to reveal it in advance, but to order it. This happens when we stand in the present, free of the restraints and fears of the past, yet filled with the creative possibilities and hopes anticipated by past promises. Being thus free to decide and to meet the future enables us to put value on our decisions, to reject some and select others, and to place goals before them. No longer is the future an endless row of confusing enigmas, but it is a constant stream of possibilities. It is being ordered.

The Middle of Time

Finally, can worship on the day of rest really produce such a response and offer us such possibilities in life? It seems to me that it can. Coming as it does at the end of the week of work and before a new week, it affords us with the occasion to look back upon the past, not in the way a teacher may look back upon the past of a student at examination time, but to look back in complete freedom. The activities of the past workweek, whether painful failures or proud moments of success, are set aside by being put in order and thus integrated into our present

85

experience. This can only happen in the lull of the battle of life provided by the day of rest when time provides the occasion for the holy to appear. Thereby our past is ordered, and we are free to make new decisions and face new possibilities in the future. The holy time of the day of rest, therefore, does not stand over against all other times to condemn them and their secular activities. Rather holy time stands in the midst of all time to order it. The reading of scripture, preaching of the word, prayers, confessions, hymns, and offerings—whatever belongs to our worship—must contribute to this ordered response to the appearance of holiness in time. No holy mountain or tree or spring or altar or temple or even a priest can so stand in the midst of all our time and set it in order. Only holy time invokes such a response in worship as puts order into our time and thus into our life. The day of rest provides the foremost occasion for such worship.

8
Time For Meditation

Stillness

In her splendid book *Out of Africa,* Isak Dinesen describes the stillness on the African steppes.

> Out in the wilds I had learned to beware of abrupt movements. The creatures with which you are dealing there are shy and watchful, they have a talent for evading you when you least expect it. No domestic animal can be as still as a wild animal. The civilized people have lost the aptitude of stillness, and must take lessons in silence from the wild before they are accepted by it. The art of moving quietly, without suddenness, is the first to be studied by the hunter, and more so by the hunter with a camera. Hunters cannot have their way, they must fall in with the wind, and the colours and smells of the landscape, and they must make the tempo of the ensemble their own. Sometimes it repeats a movement over and over again, and they must follow up with it.[1]

Stillness belongs to nature, but like the bald eagle, the blue whale, and many other natural wonders, it is threatened with extinction. Noise and restlessness are products of civilization, and they are on the increase. In fact, stillness, like so many endangered species, is left with but few remaining reserves in this world where it can still flourish.

87

Some people do not miss stillness in the least. They consider our active, restless, noisy life to be an important part of American (Western) culture—part of what makes our society work—but many thoughtful individuals are seriously concerned with the demise of stillness in our world, and they raise protest against what to them is the prospect of a nightmare: a teeming, noisy, restless mob of people pressing into every corner of the world.[2] Most such protests are directed against the largely unattended population explosion, against our insistence upon covering large areas of the earth with concrete, or against the accompanying bustle of concentrated activity and noise. But the protest is difficult and ambiguous, for nearly everyone (including many protesters) are quite committed to our existent noisy and restless civilization. At best, we may hope to lower the decibels and to slow down the proliferation of restless movement. Perhaps the operation of the noisy Concorde plane will be limited, but the general aircraft industry is bent on expanding. Perhaps the exhaust of the combustion engine will become cleaner, but the number of automobiles in operation is certain to keep increasing in the forseeable future. It is therefore not likely that noise and restlessness will suddenly vanish from our world. At best it may be somewhat curtailed and managed, at worst it will destroy us. Meanwhile, a need and longing for stillness remain unfulfilled in the life of many people.

Meditation: A Way to Be Still

The popularity of Transcendental Meditation in recent years is a testimony to that need and longing on the part of a large sector of the population. The Maharishi Mahesh

Yogi, founder of the movement, is a metaphysician trained in physics from the University of Allahabad in India. His message, which matured during time spent alone in a cave in the Himalayas and during pilgrimages in the forests of southern India, is that everyone is a distinct personal being who is capable of reaching such spiritual insight and serenity as normally is considered union with God through a set of simple meditation procedures. That this essentially "foreign gospel" has gained such wide acceptance among large number of Americans may well be attributed to their need of stillness.[3] It offers a religion without the social trappings of official Christendom to people who are starved of any spirituality, and it promises something more to life than activity, movement, and restlessness.

In the process of being transplanted to America, Transcendental Meditation has become thoroughly acclimatized to the ways of the West. It is advertised and marketed in easy steps for mass consumption. Apparently neutral observers generally agree, however, that too great claims are made for it, but they admit that the moments of stillness and synthesis that such meditation provides may do some good to some people, though it may also produce harmful or at least distressing effects in others.[4] The point of this conclusion is that Transcendental Meditation is one among several possible ways to fulfill the need of "putting it all together." Our suggestion in this chapter is that the day of rest—another institution that also originated in the East—provides in its own way a fulfillment of our need to be still. Taken at face value, the day of rest is as remarkable and as radical a solution to our need of stillness as any form of meditation. It is a great pity that its potentials, which are so readily available in our Christian biblical heritage, have been so poorly explored, but that only confirms what we have frequently experienced: the best solutions often lie closest at hand.[5]

Day of Rest: A Time for Meditation

To speak of the time for meditation that the day of rest can provide is not to suggest that this day necessarily invites some kind of formal meditation but that its special time offers experiences and benefits akin to those that are commonly attributed to meditation but without some of the stigmata of the latter. The day of rest is concerned with the individual and his need now and again to step back from the rush of life and to take his bearings. This day cares about the individual person by giving him an opportunity to mend his spirit. What enables the day of rest to offer these benefits is its quality of "private time," a quality that can enrich the meaning of all our time. We will now consider this quality of private time on the day of rest in further detail.

Time to Be Alone

First, the day of rest provides an opportunity to be alone. Many people may well consider this a decided drawback of this day, but perhaps less so if a clear distinction is made between being alone and being lonely. Loneliness is not one of the sabbath's qualities. On the contrary. Every biblical reference to this day has a social context. The sabbath is surrounded by people—people tired from long hours of work, people oppressed under heavy obligations and responsibilities, joyous people, and confident people. As we have seen, all classes are represented—both sexes, all ages, every nationality. Jesus summed it up in his famous dictum: "The sabbath was made for man, not man for the sabbath" (Mark 2:27). Not only does the sabbath have a social context throughout, it fosters social involvement and concern with people. Loneliness has no place in it.

But being alone is different from loneliness. Loneliness is painful and unnatural for people, and the day of rest vigorously counteracts it. But being alone is another matter. We will define it as being an individual, a person, a self. Someone standing over against a crowd is alone, and that is a crucial part of human experience. Various forms of meditation, we noted, have met with great popularity because of their ability to bring an individual face to face with himself. The day of rest provides a similar experience by giving us a chance to be alone. That can happen when all work is set aside and every duty is laid down. To achieve it involves stepping aside, backing off, being still. Also the worship which this day invites is performed alone though it may occur in the context of a congregation (Isa. 1:12-13). To retreat from work and to enter worship makes one alone and brings one face to face with oneself.

The experience of being alone may be illustrated by the experience of retiring, when suddenly forty to forty-five years of work come to an end. The daily routine is broken, responsibilities are gone, pressures are off. Sad to say, many retired persons find this experience very lonely, even depressing, perhaps because the many years of work were not fulfilling or productive. Ideally, retirement should not produce loneliness, but it does bring a chance to be alone—away from the weight of accomplishments (or failures), out from under the pressure, free of the demands of full-time work. It should be a time of assessment and self-examination when the accumulated experiences of life can be reviewed and put to new and creative use. Traditionally, societies have given retired members of the community important roles as counselors for these very reasons. A good counselor must know how to be alone so as to observe matters from a distance. To do so is not easy. It requires one to bear again the heavy burden of past failures and to refrain from being enticed by the glory of such successes as may have accumulated. It demands fairness to past colleagues and goodwill to successors. Many retired persons have faltered in these requirements of being alone and have chosen instead to remain (actually or imaginatively) in the crowd, often at the cost of great loneliness. "No one listens to me anymore" is the complaint of many retired persons who wish to remain in the business of life. But those few who have the courage and the ability to be alone have found both listeners and followers, and loneliness has vanished. Perhaps the experience of being alone on the day of rest is not only illustrated by the experience of retirement; it may even contribute to a satisfying and fruitful retirement.

Time to Discover Oneself

Second, by teaching us to be alone, the day of rest enables us to look at ourselves and to understand what we see. The purpose of true meditation is precisely that: a time for reflection and self-understanding, not an occasion to escape from ourselves. One criticism of Transcendental Meditation in its Westernized form is that so often it has become just a tonic that will spirit us away from all the pressures of life into a state of absolute bliss.[6] The day of rest has been similarly misunderstood, as if it were a day of escape from the world. Jewish freedom fighters during the Maccabean wars (167-164 B.C.) at one stage refused to fight on this day thinking mistakenly (we may presume) that by observing it strictly, the war would be made to go away on this day or they would be spared of any harm (I Macc. 2:29-41).

This, of course, is a gross misunderstanding. The sabbath is not a day of escape from the world, but a day of freedom before the world—freedom to be oneself. The famous sabbath reference in Isaiah 58:13 demonstrates this point in a dramatic way. It appears at the end of a section dealing with social responsibility and personal integrity. Apparently, the Jerusalem worshipers sought an escape from oppressing conditions by resorting to religious activities, and they were puzzled when their conditions did not improve (Isa. 58:3). At this, the prophet instructed them that instead of escaping from the world into religion, they might let religion loose in the world, thus making it a religion of service. Then, to the surprise of many interpreters, the sabbath is introduced, presumably as an illustration of the foregoing argument.[7] It is a well-chosen illustration, for the sabbath with its work prohibition provides an easy excuse to escape from the world, but that ought not to be. Therefore, the prophet warns against making this day a religious occasion to seek personal advantage. But more than that, the text, which is difficult to translate, makes repeated references to the sabbath observer (your foot, pleasure, ways, etc.).[8] It means to make him reassess his own attitude toward life (activities, ways, pleasures, business, etc.), by setting aside his own interests in favor of the larger good. Moreover, since the sabbath (as the seventh day of rest) sums up all our past activities, it is natural that it should provide us with an invitation to assess them.

In this sense, the day of rest is a time for seeking understanding. Not only does the completion of all work before this day provide an opportunity to look back upon it and assess it, but moreover, the goal of our work, which is implied in its completion, helps us to catch a clearer glimpse of ourselves: Had the goal of the past week's work any reasonable correspondence to the opportunities of the week? Was the goal worthy of these opportunities? Was it reached? These are personal questions, concerned not so much with the activities of the week as with the person who undertook them. He can now stand back and look at himself.

Great leaders as well as many thoughtful people will often resort to a retreat at regular intervals while ordinary mortals might join the weekend crowd on the slopes or at the beaches. Jefferson's Monticello, Roosevelt's Warm Springs, and Eisenhower's Camp David are such places of retreat to which a person faced with heavy responsibilities may retire for the purpose of self-assessment. We might naturally assume that a genuine retreat is a place designed to take busy people away from it all for a while, but that is only partially true. A retreat that enables us to escape the world completely can leave us in a worse way than before, whereas a retreat that enables us to step aside for a while to look at it all and at ourselves can send us back into life with renewed energy and fresh visions.

The day of rest is such a retreat in time. On this day we can regularly step aside and catch a glimpse of ourselves, our goals, methods, motives—but that is not all.

Time to Understand Ourselves

Third, the day of rest not only enables us to see ourselves as we have been left by the hands of the past

working week; it also gives us a chance to consider our potential for the future. It is a well-known fact that a man is known not so much by his achievements as by his potential. Writing about his grandfather who committed suicide, André Malraux wondered about the motives behind such an act. What drove the old man to his "misadventure?" asks Malraux. Why did his last wish mention a nonreligious funeral before it was finally changed by a simple, apparently last minute, correction into a request for a religious funeral? We shall never know, comments Malraux, because "essentially a man is what he hides,"[9] or put differently, a man's past life reveals less about his character than does his future potential. Man is an unfinished being, and understanding him requires that we assess the possibilities and the potentials before him, for these make him into what he really is just as much as (or even more than) the achievements he has left behind. No man is understood by simply considering what has gone before but by assessing what he is capable of doing or likely to become.

It is not surprising, therefore, that meditation which aims at self-understanding has as its stated goal the realization of human potential. It may be expressed in terms of self-fulfillment or of union with God, but its concern is with human potential. Does the day of rest in any way share this concern?

Professor Hans W. Wolff has suggested that the day of rest stands at the beginning of the workweek, not at its conclusion.[10] In this way the workweek does not consist of a steep uphill climb climaxing in a time of rest at its end; rather the week starts from the top (time of rest) and coasts downward from there. Unfortunately, such an ideal situation does not correspond with the experience of most people, nor is it supported by our biblical heritage of the sabbath that occurs everywhere at the conclusion of the week. Nevertheless, the day of rest does point forward, but only in the sense that the week will be accomplished on it. Because of this, something new is in fact anticipated on the day of rest. A new leaf is turned, but what shall be written on it? What possibilities lie ahead, and what is our potential of achieving them? The answer to these questions are buried deep inside, at the fountain of our selfhood. They must be uncovered, and the day of rest—the time for meditation—can help us to uncover them. On this day we can step aside from our busy activities, look at ourselves, examine our goals, our motives, and our past achievements, and then as we turn over a new leaf to consider our potential and the possibilities before us—that which really makes us what we are—we shall stare ourselves in the face, penetrate behind the superficiality of our busy exterior, and we shall know our own soul. We shall never understand ourselves simply by contemplating what was done in the past; we shall really know ourselves only by realizing our potential in the future, and this realization brings us very near the experience that Christians have long called communion with God. Such communion has always had one basic objective: to discover our potential in the light of God's accomplishments. The day of rest as explained by the Old Testament creation story (Gen. 2-3) and by our Lord in the Gospels (*cf.,* Mark 2:27-28; Luke 13:1 18) is a continual reminder of what God has accomplished. It therefore also presents us with a constant challenge to discover the potential before us, which is to discover ourselves.

The day of rest then gives us stillness in life, like the stillness in the wilds of creation. In it we may emerge from the busy lives with which we have surrounded ourselves, as a rare gazelle, long considered extinct, emerges from the grass of the steppe. Also, God emerges in such stillness when all our own accomplishments (successful or otherwise) are set aside in favor of his and of the potential before us. To discover God and ourselves in this stillness is the object of meditation. The day of rest provides us with both the time and the setting for such meditation, and in doing so it can profoundly affect all our time.

9
Time For Others

Time and the Christian Graces

"He/she took time for me" is one of the finest compliments anyone can receive. Ludwig Koehler once suggested that such a compliment would be accepted as testimony before the judgment throne of God![1] And indeed, our Lord himself admitted as much when he announced, "Come, O blessed of my Father, inherit the kingdom prepared for you from the foundation of the world; for . . . I was a stranger and you welcomed me, . . . I was sick and you visited me, I was in prison and you came to me" (Matt. 25:34-36). Of course, our Lord also mentioned food, drink, and clothing in this passage, but it seems that most of us find it easier to supply those material commodities than time to the least of his needy brethren. And that takes us to the rather simple thesis of this chapter: the day of rest gives us a lesson in taking time for others. But first, is that a needed lesson?

Time Shortage

It has become painfully obvious to many observers of our society that its material affluence is accompanied by a poverty in time, that our responsibility toward others is nearly always met with material things, not time, and that the needs in our society are so often related to a lack of time not material. Illustrations of this abound.

Children are robbed of parental time more frequently than of parental material support. "Dad, you did so much for me, but hardly anything with me" is the pathetic cry of a lost child. In reality, these two responses to a child's needs are undoubtedly related: parents who are aware of spending too little time with their children will often attempt to compensate for that neglect by an over-indulgency with material support—thoroughly spoiling their children with things, while starving them of time. The consequence of such parental neglect can be very serious. Children will learn less from their home than they otherwise could. Sensitive teachers become aware of this problem. The ensuing loss does not only involve practical skills (many of which can barely be taught in the urban or suburban environments in which so many children are brought up). Far more crucial is the loss of experiences in understanding and solving problems of a personal nature, such as the experience of resolving a misunderstanding or of handling a frustration. Turning to another area, a recent investigation of premarital sexual behavior reported, as expected, an increase in sexual activity among the thirteen to seventeen year olds and noted, moreover, that the family home has replaced the car and the lover's lane as the preferred place of such sexual exploits within this age group.[2] The report explained that parents are increasingly more likely to leave teen-agers at home alone during family holidays or even alone in other rooms during family gatherings. In still another area, the gap between generations about which so much was said and written a few years ago, often looms most prominently among the affluent sector of society, suggesting that not material possessions or things but something else is responsible for bringing people together. Our suggestion is that this something else takes time and has been woefully neglected, not least among the active affluent classes of society.

Married people have also become victims of the general shortage of time for others in our society. While many factors contribute to the increase in the divorce rate, lack of time is prominent among them, according to my own pastoral experience, and it has had a marked influence upon existant marriages as well, making them less personable and more vulnerable to disintegration. A marriage relationship between two people who have little or no time for each other becomes a (perhaps convenient) arrangement for providing food, shelter, some mutual services, and sex, but not an experience in personal relationship, growth, and creativity. Sex manuals recognize the need for time in marriage and urge that sex must be given time. Our concern, however, is to take time for the other, and from a Christian perspective it would be quite appropriate to suggest that a successful marriage requires time for a variety of time-consuming activities among which are work, play, conversation, sex, and sheer physical and spiritual closeness.

Especially tragic is our inability to spend time with the aged whose slow-down leaves them far behind in the mad race of life. As a medical social worker with special responsibilities for geriatrics, my wife has made me acutely aware of this problem, but it has also become a widely recognized national concern.[3] Elderly people in nursing homes far from children and grandchildren may suffer physical discomfort due to poor health-care facilities, but those sufferings are often quite small compared to the dull pain of receiving no time from others. The nurses are kind, but too busy, and members of the family often live far away. The result: no one takes time for the aged.

Now, it must be admitted that taking time for others is sometimes neither easy nor pleasant. Spending time with children can be noisy and nerve-wracking, teen-agers are often disrespectful or disinterested, even toward those who mean them well, one's spouse can be so well known and commonplace with few surprises that it becomes tempting to slip over to the "boys" or down to the club or in with a friend. Old people are not always grateful for the time that may generously be given to them. They are known to complain much and to tax our patience. Yet to spend time for others is a valuable experience: it can become life-giving to the lonely and rewarding to those who are prepared to give of their time. Where can such time be found?

The Day of Rest Is for Others

The day of rest has many attributes, among them is the time it provides for others. This attribute it inherited from the biblical sabbath. For example, the sabbath laws repeatedly emphasize that its blessing of time is for others, servants, alien laborers, children, and even domestic animals (Exod. 23:12; Deut. 5:14).

Our Lord singled out this attribute of the sabbath with painful clarity. The matter arose when he healed chronically ill people on this day. That caused controversy. The opponents of Jesus did not object to doing good on the sabbath toward people who were ill,[4] who needed circumcision,[5] or who otherwise were facing special difficulties.[6] Even the needs of animals received attention on the sabbath (see Luke 13:15; 14:5). But in every instance the sabbath time devoted to others was provided in response to a religious or ethical obligation that could be said to overrule the commandment not to work on the day of rest.[7] Jesus, on the other hand, took time for others on the sabbath without seeking any recognized religious or ethical authority to do so. A case in point is his healing of the chronically ill woman who had suffered for eighteen years. As noted above, the ruler of her synagogue objected promptly: "There are six days on which work ought to be done; come on these and be healed, and not on the sabbath day" (Luke 13:14). Jesus did not respond by referring to the common practice of rescuing a trapped animal, for after eighteen years his patient was hardly trapped in an acute need that demanded urgent attention; she was simply in need. Instead, he reminded his audience of their kindly practice of loosing ox and ass and leading them to water on the sabbath (v. 15). The woman's case was similar: she was bound and in need, and the sabbath, argued Jesus, is meant to provide time to meet such a need. Not only is it permissible to take such sabbath time for others, it is demanded. In the words of Jesus, "And ought not this woman, a daughter of Abraham whom Satan bound for eighteen years, be loosed from this bond on the sabbath day?" (v. 16). Apparently Jesus placed immense importance upon taking time for others on this day. To do so fulfills the commission of the gospel, and Jesus assumed authority over the sabbath to press it into the service of the gospel in this way (Mark 2:28).

Finally, sabbath worship distinguishes this day as a time for others. On the surface it might appear that worship time is devoted to God—and indeed it does take time to offer our deepest devotion to God, but the Old Testament prophets press home relentlessly the point that for worship (including sabbath worship) to be acceptable to God, it must be ethically responsible. Isaiah 56 is most telling. Here are worshipers who have no time for foreigners and eunuchs of whom the Assyrian and Babylonian wars produced many. This neglect is carried out in the name of religion (see Deut. 23), and the prophet will have none of it. The house of God shall be a house of prayer for all peoples (Isa. 56:7) with special attention given to those individuals who require it most: foreigners who lack friends, home, and a sense of belonging, and eunuchs who are permanently deprived of descendants. The sabbath has time especially for such, and that is the heritage passed on to the day of rest.

Finding Time on the Day of Rest

How can the day of rest help us to find time for others? By the nature of the case the answers to this question will be simple and happy ones, drawn from the experiences of life.

(a) *Time to get together.* First, the day of rest brings people together. Work scatters people in many directions and into different areas of interest. Rest from work brings them together. For many centuries traditional Jewish families have gathered around the lighted candles to open the sabbath. Such gatherings were seen not as a heavy obligation but as a welcome appointment, sometimes symbolized by an audience with a queen or by a meeting with one's bride.[8] But even without such traditional customs the day of rest brings the family together. Traveling salesmen drive home, tired laborers set down their tools, tattered homemakers put the house and themselves in order, children return from play, all gather around a day, but what does attract them to this day? Is it tasty meals? Hours of relaxation? Or the joy of seeing someone again? Undoubtedly, but more than all these it is the time which on this day we are invited to give unselfishly to others.

(b) *Time for children.* Parents will take time for their children. The heavy pressures of work are usually responsible for robbing children of parental time, though sometimes social obligations come in the way too; but on the day of rest no such pressure exists. Of course, that in itself does not guarantee children a share of parental time. I have seen careful observers of the day of rest hoard this free time egotistically rather than sharing it. But the day does at least make time available and urges that it be shared with others. It is indeed a happy sight to see parents and children spending time together on the day of rest. My own childhood is full of memories of times in the company of my father at the beach, in the forest, walking, driving, talking, and exploring. Afterward, at the supper table, a guest once commented to my father in our hearing that he was spending a lot of his spare time with his three boys. At this my father thought for a long time, then commented, "What else should I do with it?" The impact of such time, most of which occurred on the day of rest, can have a marked impact on all subsequent times.

(c) *Time for one other person.* The ancient Jewish teachers were somewhat puzzled by the question of taking time for others on the day of rest. On the one hand this day seemed to them an important occasion for married people to spend in each other's company, but on the other hand, they worried about profaning the holy day with too "human" activities. This ambivalence is reflected in the, to us, amusing rules regarding marriage relations on the day of rest. The strict school of Judaism forbade conjugal relations on this day on the grounds that such would distract from its sanctity, whereas the more liberal school of rabbis allowed (even urged) such relations because they would enhance the joy of this day and make it an occasion for loving care of one other person.[9] Few Christians would be concerned with such considerations today. In fact, the consensus of opinion in the many marriage manuals on the market seems to be that any time is a good time to enjoy one's marriage. But this nearly misses the crucial problem in our marriage relationship today, and that is not to select a time together but to find *any time at all,* not just for sex, but for such personal fellowship and interaction that characterizes a good marriage relation and of which sex is meant to be an intimate, rather delicate, and deeply personal expression.

The problem of marriage is to find time to break the estrangement between husband and wife whose paths cross more often than they parallel. So again in this area the day of rest provides time for others, and those open-minded rabbinic teachers who urged husbands and wives to spend time together had well captured the spirit of this day. That two people who care about each other should need time together is so obvious that I am hard put to understand why so few have taken advantage of the time provided them on this occasion. The day of rest not only sets time aside, it also reaches back into its biblical heritage and fills this time with selfless care for others. That care can be expressed in many ways: sharing of necessary duties, conversation, walk, play, laughter, meeting of minds, and closeness of body and soul.

(d) *Time for the aged.* "In the life of every little boy there ought to be an old man" goes the saying. Unfortunately, we often separate the young from the old, which is quite an unnatural arrangement. I never cease to be amazed at the interest that older people in nearby nursing homes take in my young son who, after all, is a total stranger to them. Similarly, children have far more patience with the old than many grown-ups demonstrate, and they are generally fascinated by the many curious things from another age with which old people always seem to be surrounded. We are the guilty ones who have no time for the old. We place them in comfortable nursing homes, but without the comfort of seeing a child playing or an adult working. We have no time to listen to their stories or to let them see the progress of the life that they began. The day of rest is kind to the aged. On this day our work and all the things that keep us so busy stops and slows us down to the speed of those who rest. On this day the old find affinity with the young, and the young can share the experience of the old. The day of rest invites us to share kindness toward the old by stopping to listen to them, to pay them a visit, to send a message, or to bring them out of their isolation. Such times taken for others can infuse new life and energy into the otherwise dull existence of an old person (perhaps a grandparent), and it also teaches us a lesson about our own life which must face the specter of old age one day.

(e) *Time for others.* The Bible often speaks of the "stranger within your gates" in the content of the day of rest. Time must be also given to him on this day, but how can we respond to this command? Who are the strangers in our midst? So often the day of rest is spent in our comfortable backyards, in the garden chairs, or around the patio barbecue. Do not the quiet hours of our day of rest give us an opportunity to let our homes and backyards be places where strangers can refresh themselves? Used this way our day of rest will become an oasis in time, a quiet period in which travelers may settle in our presence and take advantage of the time which we can give them.

As a student traveling among the farms in Scotland with religious books, I often enjoyed such quiet times in someone's home. Surely, these farmers were busy during the summer months, and I was a total stranger to them, even a foreigner, yet they took time for me. "Come in and sit down by the fire," was the invitation from many a small cottage, "it is just about time for tea." "Stay with us over the weekend and visit our church," they would say. "Let us go into the sitting room," a titled gentleman once announced, and there he related to me a story of his ancestors that ran like a thumbnail sketch of the British Empire from Gibraltar to Calcutta. But best of all I recall the pleasant hours of the day of rest, walking down main street to the kirk (church) with young and old, meeting the congregation after the service, eating lunch with hospitable and generous people, and sitting by the fire with my host listening to him tell the tale of his town. These people recognized a stranger within their gate and found time for him.

Time and Things

One of the very obvious consequences of our affluent society is that we fulfill our philanthropic obligations to others with our means rather than with our time. Poorer people in other societies express their concern for others

107

by taking time for them, but for us it is easier to bring a donation or to mail off a hastily written postcard to someone in need. We give that of which we have most—money and things. But the world and its people have a crying need of time—time to communicate, time to grow up, time to share, time to be heard and to talk, time to touch and to linger in someone's presence, time to live, time to cry, time to rest, yes, even time to die. How can we even begin to meet this need? The day of rest teaches us to give what is most needed, namely, time, but more than that, it actually enables us once a week to take some time for others. It could even make us philanthropists with time.

10
Time For The Future

Contending with the Future

The future is the concern of dreamers, planners, and prophets, and all three have found it a troublesome subject. Dreams often do not come true, plans fail or must be revised, and as for prophets, said Storm P. in gentle sarcasm; "It is difficult to prophecy—especially about the future."[1] Yet despite these difficulties the future commands a powerful spell over many people. To some it holds a promise of better things to come, to others it hides a threat of misfortune, while to still others it represents an endless continuation of a hopeless (and often miserable) existence. In every instance the future is understood in terms of the present. The optimist looks for a future improvement of the present and believes to have detected positive signs of it, the pessimist shudders before the future fearing some unforeseen upset of present favorable (or at least tolerable) conditions, while the fatalist resigns himself to the inevitable, that the present will continue into the future with no real possibility of molding it and little chance of bettering it.

At times when the future looks particularly precarious we close our eyes to it altogether, and that, perhaps, is the most pitiful of all approaches to the future. George, whom I met in Hamilton, New South Wales, Australia,

109

illustrates such an attitude to the future. He had immigrated from Greece with his common-law wife, two children, and two "brothers-in-law" to build a glorious future in a new land of promise and opportunity. It meant hard work for the men of this little family in the nearby steel works. Their earnings, except for George's, were pooled and set aside toward the purchase of a house. George was the outsider, and his paycheck went to support the communal kitchen. After a year George fell ill and visited the physician whose language he could not speak. A superficial diagnosis pointed to stomach trouble, and a simple drugstore medication was prescribed, but to no avail. A second visit to the physician rendered the same result, while George grew steadily worse. Finally, his physician took the case seriously and from then on events followed in rapid succession: hospitalization, tests, x-rays, exploratory surgery, incurable cirrhosis (liver ailment), painkillers, visits from his now near-hysterical and guilt-ridden family, and thoughts about the future. The surgeon knew his patient's future, but could not speak with him, and what he did get across was not accepted. At this point, my social-worker wife was put on the case to make George's future unmistakably clear: four to six months at the most. But no one in his family really believed that. Friends invited George home to rest (and get well), plans were made for his return to Greece, his car (the only real possession he had) was sold, church donations accumulated, and friends and concerned people beat a steady path to his little attic room to wish him well. That is where I met him. Visitors were speaking softly, moving in and out of the room whispering messages to each other. George appeared cheerful, and his friends joked about his prowess, but they handled him like a child. Everyone played the act (of

110

the death scene), but no one believed the script. His friends spoke (seriously) about super-physicians in Greece, of liver transplants, and of faulty diagnosis (it is a stomach ulcer, just like Uncle Nick's). George, himself, pretended cheerfully that he was getting better and had managed the whole day without painkillers, though his glass of pills was half empty and his friends knew that he ate them like candy when left alone in the room.

That was our last visit. We will not meet George again. But his blindfolded attitude to the future made a striking impression upon my mind. It is an attitude that is shared by many others who have much less reason for doing so. In fact, the history of our civilization has revealed a persistent blindness toward the future. A case in point is the firm belief held by many people that our future supply of fossil energy will be as adequate as our present supply, even though our senses tell us that it must be limited even as the earth itself is limited. But the larger point is this: our view of the future is often sadly limited by our present experiences. How can this limitation be broken and our future opened up?

Facing the Future on the Day of Rest

The thesis of this chapter is that the day of rest invites us to reassess the relationship between present and future and that by participating in the present experience of this day, the future will emerge open before us anew. How can this happen?

(a) *The day that stands before us.* The day of rest always stands before us because it comes at the conclusion of our division of time into seven-day periods. At this point a fundamental difference emerges between the biblical sabbath and the Christian Sunday: The sabbath ends the week, while Sunday begins it.[2] This difference explains why the earliest Sunday was not a day of rest, but was a time to worship the risen Lord, and some evidence exists that many Christians of the third to the fifth century A.D. observed both days: Sunday for the redemption of the risen Lord and the sabbath for the rest of the Creator.[3] There simply was no precedent for observing a day of rest on the first day of the week. Only gradually, beginning perhaps in the second century and meeting with some hesitation in the third and fourth centuries A.D., was the quality of rest transferred from the sabbath to Sunday.[4] That was not a natural transfer, for it ran counter to some of the deep-seated sabbath principles associated exclusively with the last day of the week, and the whole process was difficult. It is now considered likely that developing anti-Semitic sentiments in the Roman Empire and actual persecutions of the Jews were instrumental in urging the Christians to abandon the sabbath in favor of the first day so as to distinguish clearly between themselves and the Jews.[5] Eventually, during the fourth century A.D. the transfer of the sabbath rest to Sunday was proposed in an official way. The first day of the week was decreed to be the religious day of worship in Rome by Roman Emperor Constantine, and a few years later legislation was established to make it into a Sabbath day of rest on which work was prohibited.[6]

Now it is indeed a curious fact of history that when the early Christians, for reasons of their own, ultimately rejected the sabbath day of rest for the Sunday memorial of the resurrected Lord they should retain the sabbath's quality of rest, thus making Sunday into a sabbath of sorts.[7] The resurrection event itself inspires not rest but work. The words of the resurrected Lord are: "Go and tell my brethren" (Matt. 28:10); "Go therefore and make disciples of all nations, baptizing . . . teaching" (vv. 19-20). Here is no mention of any rest or finished work. The Resurrection represents a beginning, not an end. The words "It is finished" (John 19:30) belong three days before the Resurrection, at the Crucifixion. Therefore, when Sunday, the first day of the week, eventually became also a day of rest it adopted a foreign element that really belongs to the sabbath. That demonstrates the importance of the sabbath principle in the Christian communion. Christians, it was discovered, as well as Jews, need the experience of rest from work, a rest that comes at the end of work and therefore a rest that is always before us. That quality of the day of rest turns our attention away from the present and into the future in a number of different ways.

(b) *The day that becomes a goal.* The day of rest characterizes the future as the goal of the present. This means that not only does the present stand waiting before the future to see what it might bring but also the future stands before the present instructing it about its goal. Our point is that when the future stands before the present in this way it stands dressed in the day of rest.

The biblical day of rest (the sabbath) also functioned in this way anciently. It became, as it were, the embodiment of Israel's future by means of its quality of rest. At this point, rest takes on extraordinary proportions, referring not only to rest from servitude but also to rest from the struggles of life that, in the case of Israel, means rest in the promised land and particularly the accompanying spiritual rest in God's redemption. This is the intention of Joshua 21:43-45.

Thus the LORD gave to Israel all the land which he swore to give to their fathers; and having taken possession of it, they settled there. And the LORD gave them rest on every side just as he has sworn to their fathers; not one of all their enemies had withstood them, for the LORD had given all their enemies into their hands. Not one of all the good promises which the LORD had made to the house of Israel had failed; all came to pass.

It is well known to Bible readers that Israel did not immediately achieve such rest. The independence wars continued during the time of the judges and had to be resumed repeatedly during the monarchy. Rest from their enemies might occur from time to time, but never permanently so that Israel could claim to have achieved it.[8] Consequently, the future (symbolized by rest) continued to stand before Israel as a promise as well as a threat. The threat is that Israel will never enter this rest, as suggested by the psalmist: "Therefore I swore in my anger that they should not enter my rest" (Ps. 95:11). The promise, on the other hand, assures not that the people of Israel will find rest but that the rest will find its people. Both the Chronicler and the psalmist affirms this assurance with the promise that although the nation may not find rest in the land, God will find rest among his people (see II Chron. 6:4-6; Ps. 132:13).

Such a rest cannot be fulfilled in casual moments of sublime spiritual quietude or in comfortable physical relaxation. Rather, it represents the goal of all God's creation and of every truly human endeavor. It represents the future that stands before our present, instructing it and inviting it forward. Our Lord himself spoke of his future as a rest in the words which Bertil Thorvaldsen has immortalized in sculpture:[9] "Come to me, all who labor and are heavy laden, and I will give you rest" (Matt.

114

11:28). This is no sentimental invitation to "smother in the bosom of Jesus," for he continues: "Take my yoke upon you" (v. 29). Rather, the new life of discipleship to which our Lord calls his followers—though burdened with the pain of a cross—can be considered a rest because it represents the future standing before all past and present efforts calling them to their fulfillment.

It is perhaps important to observe that the very next verse in Matthew's Gospel (12:1) introduces the day of rest (Jesus allowing his disciples to gather grain on the sabbath and healing a withered hand on this day). Perhaps we are to understand these sabbath incidents as illustrations of the foregoing discussion of rest. If so, his rest is again characterized not by inactivity but by the fulfillment of all activity.

Our own days of rest can serve us in this same way, not just in the practical way of setting a temporal limit to our work and a goal before it, but by placing an ideal before us—an ideal of the future, of completed work, and of a goal reached, not in violence, oppression, or dominance, but in a rest of peace and harmony. Such is the future which the day of rest represents.

(c) *The day that inspires creativity.* Because the day of rest points to a fulfillment of our present it is concerned with creativity. Materially speaking, to create means to make something from nothing (*ex nihilo*), but temporally speaking, to create means to complete something so that it can be said that what is created does not need further work: not only is it made from nothing, but it is completely made into something.

The story of creation in the Bible makes this distinction clearly. First the Creator made something (animals, sun, plants, etc.) by the sheer force of his word—no raw material was required—and then he completed the creation by pronouncing it very good (Gen. 1:3, 31). In a similar way the day of rest, which was introduced at the conclusion of creation (2:2-3), testifies to the fact that creation is both accomplished (God finished) and fulfilled (God sanctified and blessed). The day of rest also stands before our works urging that they be done creatively—accomplished and fulfilled.

It is a great pleasure for men and women to live and work creatively. Not only does that remove the drudgery from life, but it gives a sense of satisfaction, yet with no cause for pride. A farmer may experience this when his fields are well planted or his crop is safely in the barn. A builder may share it when his construction stands up well and on schedule. A teacher may have the rare satisfaction of seeing his students firmly in command of a subject. Of course, not all our work is done creatively, perhaps most of it is not, but however unsuccessful we may be at times, the vision of a task well completed need never be lost. That is the vision of creativity. Once that vision is lost, man descends to the level of the animal. He may still eat, work, and propagate; he may experience both pain and pleasure, but he will not have a future, for that requires man to project himself imaginatively into his completed works. The day of rest stands before him as a symbol of the future by inspiring such creativity.

(d) *Celebration anticipates the future.* By virtue of its celebration the day of rest participates in the future in still another way.[10] Celebration is a particular human activity without which our response to the world with all its delights and repulsiveness cannot be complete. "Man," wrote Walter Harrelson, "cannot live a fully human life without acts of celebration."[11]

116

Of course, not all acts of celebration are concerned with the future. Celebrations also look back, perhaps in thanksgiving or in repentance. It also meets present circumstances as in the case of grief (at a funeral) when the loss of life must somehow be integrated into the continuation of life among those left behind. But above all else, celebration looks forward by relishing the possibilities that lie ahead. This is obviously true about celebrations of life, as at the birth of a child or at a wedding, but even funerals have a forward glance toward the still untold fruits to be reaped from a life well lived or toward the resurrection hope. In short, when we truly celebrate we may look in many directions but never without also casting our eyes forward into the future.

Curiously, the celebration on the day of rest has traditionally taken us back to creation (Exod. 20:11) and to Israel's Exodus redemption (Deut. 5:15) or even to the risen Lord (as in the case of Sunday observance). Yet the very nature of our celebration on this day, though it takes us back, quickly turns our attention forward. Celebrating the completed creation is only a small step removed from celebrating the potential blessing and sanctification which meets the celebrant. Similarly, celebrating God's past acts of redemption inevitably takes us to the future potentials of this divine work. Celebrating on the day of rest remembers the past and anticipates the future.

Clever people have long attempted to plan for the future, sometimes with a measure of success. To do so requires many skills, among them calculation, estimation, second guessing, and a clear sense of direction. Shrewd business executives attempt such planning, and on a smaller scale most housekeepers, students, self-employed people, and others have to do the same. All project the present into the future and organize life according to these projections.

Celebrating the future by anticipating it is another matter. Here we do not project the present into the future to see what it might be like. Rather, in celebration we grasp the essence of the future, place it before us, and anticipate its reality. For example, the wedding celebration is not concerned with the period of engagement to see where it might reasonably lead. On the contrary, the wedding through its quality of celebration is able to grasp the future marriage with home, children, and so on, and to set it up as a reality that bride, groom, witnesses, and all guests can vividly anticipate. The wedding celebration encapsules the future marriage in the present. Of course, the way into the future may be obstructed by many unforeseen difficulties, even traumas, but thanks to celebration, that future has already been anticipated so that its ideals can be retained and its enigmas overcome.

Similarly, the celebration on the day of rest provides an anticipation of the future. On this day the intentions and ideals of the future can be grasped and placed before us, as it were. In this act of celebration the goal of our life, its completion, and its fulfillment are brought into view.

A Time for the Future

Viewed this way, the day of rest may be called a time for the future. It always stands before us, it calls upon the fulfillment of past and present time through creative work, and it anticipates our future through its celebration. The early Christian "pastor" who wrote the letter to the Hebrews expressed his concern for his parishioner's future by means of this principle embodied in the day of rest. His argument goes as follows (Heb. 3:7–4:10): In the beginning God gave assurance that all creation would find its fulfillment in a future experience of rest (Gen. 2:2-3), but the people of Israel spurned his assurance for the future (Ps. 95:11), leaving the promise of rest unclaimed until now. To accept that future means to claim the rest that God established at creation and whose fulfillment he promised, so the author of the letter to the Hebrews concludes: "There remains a sabbath rest for the people of God" (Heb. 4:9). This "sabbath rest" represents all the hopes and aspirations that a concerned pastor could have for his congregation of faltering Christians, because to enter it would be their only chance of facing the future which God held out for them.

Rabbi Heschel who thought much about the day of rest relates the legend about God's promise to Israel when he gave them the law. If you keep the law, he promised them, I will give you a most precious thing in my possession. And what could that be, they asked. The world to come, he replied. Show us an example of the world to come, they asked (skeptically!). The sabbath is an example of the world to come, he answered.[12] To put that story into our own words we might say that the day of rest is able in a marvelous way to encapsule the future in one moment of present time. That would perhaps be the most extraordinary contribution of the special time of the day of rest to all our time: on the day of rest we have an audience with the future.

Notes

I

1. Augustine, *Confessions*, XI, 14.
2. Lewis Carroll, *Alice's Adventures in Wonderland,* chap. 7, "A Mad Tea Party."
3. *Ibid.*
4. See for example Paul K. Jewett, *The Lord's Day* (Grand Rapids: Eerdmans, 1971), pp. 123-55; H. H. Ward, *Space-Age Sunday* (New York: Macmillan, 1960); Warren L. Johns, *Dateline Sunday, U. S. A.* (Mountain View, Calif.: Pacific Press, 1967).
5. See William F. Albright, *From the Stone Age to Christianity,* 2nd ed. (Baltimore: Johns Hopkins Press, 1957), pp. 314-19.

II

1. For a full discussion of Israel's calendars see J. van Goudoever, *Biblical Calendar,* 2nd ed. (Leiden: E. J. Brill, 1961); S. J. De Vries, "Calendar," in *Interpreter's Dictionary of the Bible,* 4 vols., ed. George A. Buttrick (Nashville: Abingdon, 1962), I, 483-88.
2. For one recent survey of this problem, see the study by this author, *The Old Testament Sabbath* (Missoula, Mont.: Society of Biblical Literature Dissertation Series, 1972), pp. 3-5, 94-101.
3. The planets would be Saturn, Mars, Mercury, Jupiter, and Venus. The Romans (and perhaps the Egyptians before them) used the names of the sun, the moon, and these planets to name the days of the week. Our English names for the days Tuesday–Friday are borrowed from the names of Nordic gods.
4. See Willy Rordorf, *Sunday,* trans. A.A.K. Graham (Philadelphia: Westminster Press, 1968), pp. 24-28.
5. See Hutton Webster, *Rest Days: A Study in Early Law and Morality* (New York: Macmillan, 1916).
6. For example, Gen. 7:4; Lev. 23:6, 34-36, 39-42; Josh. 6:4; I Sam.

11:3. See also Samuel E. Loewenstamm, "The Seven-Day Unit in Ugaritic Epic Literature," *Israel Exploration Journal,* 15 (1965), 121-33.

7. The king could not ride in his chariot, the physican could not heal, and the prophet could not give an oracle. See Stephen Langdon, *Babylonian Menologies and the Semitic Calendars* (London: Oxford University Press, 1935).

8. It appears in the Babylonian creation story *Enuma elis* (V, 18) and the flood story of *Atra-Hasis* (I, 206, 221). For the interesting similarity between *sabattu* and sabbath see Andreasen, *Old Testament Sabbath,* pp. 101-2.

9. See Exod. 23:14-17; 34:18-20, 22-24; Lev. 23:4-44; Num. 28-29; Deut. 16:1-17.

10. See Lev. 16. For a technical discussion of these festivals, see Hans-Joachim Kraus, *Worship in Israel,* trans Geoffrey Buswell (Richmond: John Knox Press, 1966).

11. See especially, Sigmund Mowinckel, *The Psalms in Israel's Worship,* 2 vols., trans. D. R. Ap-Thomas (Nashville: Abingdon, 1962), and Artur Weiser, *The Psalms,* trans. Herbert Hartwell (Philadelphia: Westminster Press, 1962).

12. Ancient Israel considered the day to begin with the evening, that is, with the night, and to conclude with the day (see Gen. 1:5).

13. The word holy (*qodes*) means "set apart." See J. Muilenburg, "Holiness," in *Interpreter's Dictionary,* II, 617.

III

1. Quoted in Richard M. Huber, *The American Idea of Success* (New York: McGraw-Hill, 1971), p. ix.

2. Jaroslav Pelikan, ed., *Luther's Works: Genesis, Chapters 1–5* (St. Louis: Concordia, 1958), vol. 1, p. 103.

3. John Calvin, *Institutes,* ed. J. T. McNeill, Library of Christian Classics (London: Oxford University Press, 1960), p. 725.

4. *Ibid.*

5. Max Weber, *The Protestant Ethic and the Spirit of Capitalism,* trans. T. Parsons (New York: Scribner's, 1958).

6. See Richard H. Tawney, *Religion and the Rise of Capitalism* (New York: Harcourt, Brace and Company, 1926).

7. See Robert W. Green, ed., *Protestantism and Capitalism and Social Science: The Weber Thesis Controversy,* Problems in American Civilization Series (Boston: Heath, 1959).

8. *Ibid.* See especially the essays by Amintore Fanfani and Albert Hyma.

9. For example in Luther's *Address to the German Nobility* and *Trade and Usury.*

10. See Robert G. Middleton, "The Protestant Principle vs. Protestant Ethic," *Christian Century,* 89 (1972), 844-46.

11. *The Wall Street Journal,* March 1, 1977, p. 1. U. S. observers from industry and research have studied the Volvo experiment since its inception.

12. This topic has played an important role in the discussion of Britain's many industrial disputes in recent years. It is also credited with the relatively calm industrial relations in West Germany and Japan.

13. See Hans. W. Wolff, *Anthropology of the Old Testament,* trans. Margaret Kohl (Philadelphia: Fortress Press, 1974), pp. 128-33.

14. *Ibid.,* p. 141.

IV

1. See "Hours of Work and Output," United States Department of Labor, Bureau of Labor Statistics, Bulletin No. 917.

2. The fact that the Muslims promoted sciences during the Middle Ages and the Communists are interested in technology are said to confirm Islam and Marxism as Judeo-Christian heresies. Lynn White, Jr., "The Historical Roots of Our Ecological Crisis," *Science,* 155 (1967), 1205.

3. *Ibid.,* pp. 1206-7.

4. Tradition has it that Francis preached to the birds, or at least got them to not interrupt his preaching, tamed a wolf, and that the fish came out of the water to hear him.

5. See Gerhard von Rad, *Genesis,* trans. J. H. Marks, Old Testament Library (London: SCM Press, 1972), p. 59f.

6. See Claus Westermann, *Genesis* (Neukirchen-Vluyn: Neukirchener Verlag, 1966–), p. 219.

7. White, "Historical Roots," p. 1203.

8. See Martin Noth, *Exodus,* trans. J. H. Marks, Old Testament Library (London: SCM Press, 1962), p. 189.

9. See Paul Tournier, ed., *Fatigue in Modern Society,* trans. James Farley (Richmond: John Knox Press, 1965).

10. "Weariness, Exile and Chaos," *Catholic Biblical Quarterly,* 34 (1971), 19-38; "Kingship and Chaos," *ibid.,* 33 (1970), pp. 317-32.

11. Viktor E. Frankl, *Man's Search for Meaning,* trans. Isle Lasch (Boston: Beacon Press, 1962), p. 108.

12. Franz Kafka, *Parables and Paradoxes* (New York: Schoken Books, 1958), p. 175.

13. Frankl, *Man's Search for Meaning,* p. 99.

V

1. Paul de Lagarde, *Deutsche Schriften.* Quoted in Helmut Thielicke, *The Freedom of the Christian Man,* trans. John W. Doberstein (New York: Harper, 1963), p. 10.

2. Wolfgang Beinert, "God—The Ground of Our Freedom," *Theology Digest,* 24 (1976), 24-25; Hans Küng, *Freedom Today,* trans. Cecily Hastings (New York: Sheed & Ward, 1965), pp. 39-46.

3. This is sometimes referred to as the Hegelian-Marxist understanding of history.

4. *The Communist Manifesto,* prepared in 1848 by Marx and Engels, concludes with an appeal for all laborers to join in this conflict with a view toward attaining freedom. "They [the Communists] openly declare that their ends can be attained only by forcible overthrow of all existing social conditions. Let the ruling classes tremble at the communist revolution. The proletarians have nothing to lose but their chains."

5. Sigmund Freud, *Inhibitions, Symptoms and Anxiety* (London, 1936). "The urge for freedom," wrote Freud, "is directed against particular forms and demands of civilization or against civilization altogether" (since these demands inhibit free and natural human behavior).

6. Herbert Marcuse, *An Essay on Liberation* (Boston: Beacon Press, 1969).

7. Abraham J. Heschel, *The Sabbath* (New York: Farrar, Straus & Giroux, 1952).

8. See chapter 4, pp. 45-48.

9. A. Falkenstein and A. von Soden, *Sumerische und akkadische Hynmen und Gebete* (Zürich: Artemis-Verlag, 1953), p. 180.

10. Küng, *Freedom Today,* pp. 2-31.

VI

1. Heschel, *The Sabbath,* p. 76.

2. Harvey Cox, *The Secular City* (New York: Macmillan, 1965), p. 261.

3. Gerhard M. Martin, *Fest: The Transformation of Everyday,* trans. M. Douglas Meeks (Philadelphia: Fortress Press, 1976), p. 21.

4. See Robert E. Neale, *In Praise of Play* (New York: Harper, 1969); David L. Miller, *God and Games: Toward a Theology of Play* (New York: Harper, 1973); Josef Pieper, *In Tune with the World: A Theory*

of Festivity, trans. Richard and Clara Winston (New York: Harcourt Brace, 1965).

5. Pieper, *In Tune with the World,* p. 20.
6. Ruben Alves, "More on Play," *Christianity and Crisis,* 32 (March 6, 1972), 46. For a fuller discussion see Alves, *Tomorrow's Child: Imagination, Creativity, and the Rebirth of Culture* (New York: Harper, 1972).
7. Gammer Gurton, "Come Play with Me," *Christianity and Crisis,* 31 (December 13, 1971), 274.
8. Martin, *Fest,* p. 30.
9. Peter Berger, *A Rumor of Angels* (New York: Irvington, 1969), pp. 72-81, 86-90; see also Harvey Cox, *The Feast of Fools* (New York: Harper, 1972).

VII

1. W. J. Harrelson, *From Fertility Cult to Worship,* (Garden City, N. Y.: Doubleday, 1969), p. 19.
2. The frequent criticism of these movements is that they are concerned primarily with congregational sanctification to the exclusion of community renewal. Thus, the "charismatic movement" has been compared to a "liturgical movement." Erling Jorstad, ed. *The Holy Spirit in Today's Church* (Nashville: Abingdon, 1973), pp. 142-43.
3. "Man is by his constitution a religious animal." Attributed to E. Burke (1730–97).
4. Cf. Martin Ebon, ed. *The Satan Trap: Dangers of the Occult* (Garden City, N. Y.: Doubleday, 1976).
5. Harrelson, *From Fertility Cult to Worship,* p. 19.
6. Talk given in Clairmont, California, 1966.
7. H. H. Rowley, *Worship in Ancient Israel* (Philadelphia: Fortress Press, 1967), p. 241.
8. Paul Tillich, *The Eternal Now* (New York: Scribner's, 1963), p. 30.
9. See chapter 1, pp. 15-19.

VIII

1. Isak Dinesen, *Out of Africa* (New York: Random House, 1965), p. 16.
2. See the (sometimes controversial) work of Stanford's Paul and Anne Ehrlich, *Population, Resources, Environment,* 2nd ed. (San Fran-

cisco: W. H. Freeman, 1972), and the shorter *Human Ecology* (San Francisco: W. H. Freeman, 1973).

3. Gary E. Schwartz, "TM Relaxes Some People and Makes Them Feel Better," *Psychology Today,* April, 1974, p. 44.

4. *Ibid. Cf.* Leon S. Otis, "If Well-Integrated but Anxious, Try TM," *ibid.,* p. 46.

5. On the relationship between the day of rest and meditation see Harvey G. Cox, *Turning East* (New York: Simon & Schuster, 1977), pp. 63-73.

6. Colin Campbell, "Transcendence Is as American as Ralph Waldo Emerson," *ibid.,* p. 38.

7. To some interpreters the sudden introduction of the sabbath in a chapter dealing with social welfare is so strange that the sabbath text is considered a secondary addition. Thus, Claus Westermann, *Isaiah 40–66,* trans. David M. Stalker, Old Testament Library (Philadelphia: Westminster Press, 1969), p. 340. In the view of J. Muilenburg, however, to remove the sabbath texts would leave the chapter a torso. See "Isaiah 40–66," *The Interpreter's Bible,* 12 vols., ed. George A. Buttrick (Nashville: Abingdon, 1952–57), V, 677.

8. The difficulty in translation lies in knowing precisely what activities are set aside on the sabbath. Apparently they are man's everyday interests and activities. For the interesting NEB translation see chap. 6, p. 72.

9. André Malraux, *Antimemoirs,* trans. Terence Kilmartin (New York: Holt, Rinehart and Winston, 1968), p. 24.

10. Hans W. Wolff, "The Day of Rest in the Old Testament," *Lexington Theological Quarterly,* 7 (1972), 69.

IX

1. Quoted in Wolff, "The Day of Rest in the Old Testament," pp. 71.

2. Reported in the *Washington Post,* April 8, 1977. The study was undertaken by John Hopkins professors M. Zelnik and J. Kantner. Details of the study were published in the monthly journal of Planned Parenthood—World Population.

3. D. Neff, "Who Killed Viola Sandberg?" *These Times,* March, 1976, pp. 3-6, is a moving dramatization of the plight of the aged in nursing homes.

4. At least one rabbinic school allowed visiting and comforting the ill on the sabbath. Strack-Billerbeck, *Kommentar Zum Neuen Testament* (Munich, 1924–61), I, 630.

5. See John 7:19-23; Strack-Billerbeck, *Kommentar,* II, 487.

6. Their principle was that any danger to life sets aside the sabbath requirement. *Ibid.,* I, 624.

7. A principle judged more important than the sabbath principle was needed to set aside the latter. For example, it was argued that if the recovery of an ill person was in doubt, the sabbath principle should not be set aside for the sake of paying him a visit. *Ibid.,* I, 624.
8. Samuel H. Dresner, *The Sabbath* (New York: Burning Bush Press, 1970), pp. 16-26.
9. See the pseudepigraphal book of Jubilees, 50, in R. H. Charles *et al., The Apocrypha and Pseudepigrapha of the Old Testament,* 2 vols. (Oxford: Clarendon Press, 1913), II, 81-82.

X

1. Source of popular Danish humor.
2. Wolff, "The Day of Rest in the Old Testament," p. 69.
3. See Jewett, *The Lord's Day,* pp. 47-48; Rordorf, *Sunday,* pp. 142-53.
4. See Rordorf, *Sunday,* pp. 142-53, 163-73; Jewett, *The Lord's Day,* pp. 123-27.
5. Samuele Bacchiocchi, *Anti-Judaism and the Origin of Sunday* (Rome: Pontifical Gregorian University Press, 1975).
6. The Edict of 313 A.D. permitted full freedom to Christianity. A second Edict of 321 A.D. prohibited work (except urgent agricultural tasks) on Sunday. See Joseph C. Ayer, *A Sourcebook for Ancient Church History* (New York: AMS Press, 1913), pp. 263, 284.
7. So called among the Puritans. See Jewett, *The Lord's Day,* pp. 151-55.
8. See Gerhard von Rad, "There Remains Still a Rest for the People of God," in *The Problem of the Hexateuch and Other Essays,* trans. E. W. Trueman Dicken (New York: McGraw-Hill, 1966), p. 97.
9. The original from which many copies have been made stands in the Church of Our Lady in Copenhagen.
10. By celebration we mean acts of worship, which may include a large spectrum of emotions from weeping to laughter.
11. Harrelson, *From Fertility Cult to Worship,* p. xiii.
12. Heschel, *The Sabbath,* p. 73.

For Further Reading

Bacchiocchi, Samuele. *From Sabbath to Sunday.* Rome: Pontifical Gregorian University Press, 1977.

Barack, Nathan A. *A History of the Sabbath.* New York: Jonathan David, 1965.

De Grazia, Sebastian. *Of Time, Work, and Leisure.* New York: Twentieth Century Fund, 1973.

Dresner, Samuel. *The Sabbath.* New York: Burning Bush Press, 1970.

Frankl, Viktor E. *Man's Search for Meaning.* Boston: Beacon Press, 1975.

Harrelson, W. J. *From Fertility Cult to Worship.* Garden City, N. Y.: Doubleday, 1969.

Heschel, Abraham J. *The Sabbath.* New York: Farrar, Straus & Giroux, 1975.

Jewett, Paul K. *The Lord's Day.* Grand Rapids: Eerdmans, 1971.

Küng, Hans. *Freedom Today.* New York: Sheed & Ward, 1966.

Martin, Gerhard M. *Fest: The Transformation of Everyday.* Philadelphia: Fortress Press, 1976.

Moltmann, Jurgen et al. *Theology of Play.* New York: Harper, 1972.

Oates, Wayne E. *Confessions of a Workaholic.* Nashville: Abingdon, 1971.

O'Toole, James, ed. *Work and the Quality of Life.* Cambridge, Mass.: MIT Press, 1974.

————. *Work in America.* Cambridge, Mass.: MIT Press, 1973.

Priestley, J. B. *Man and Time.* London: Aldus Books, Ltd., 1964.

Rordorf, Willy. *Sunday.* Philadelphia: Westminster Press, 1968.

Smigel, Edwin O., ed. *Work and Leisure.* New Haven, Conn.: College and University Presses, 1963.

Tournier, Paul, ed. *Fatigue in Modern Society.* Richmond: John Knox Press, 1965.

Ward, H. H. *Space-Age Sunday.* New York: Macmillan, 1960.

Wolff, Hans W. *Anthropology of the Old Testament.* Translated by Margaret Kohl. Philadelphia: Fortress Press, 1974, pp. 128-42.